Dream Changer

Dreams Change...
But Never Stop Dreaming

By: Jamila Phillips

Please direct all copyright inquiries to:
B.O.Y. Enterprises, Inc.
c/o Author Copyrights
P.O. Box 1012
Lowell, NC 28098

Paperback ISBN: 978-1-955605-30-4

Cover and Interior Design: B.O.Y. Enterprises, Inc.

Printed in the United States.

Dedication

To Andrew, my tenacious, curious, never mind your own business, hourly appointment reminder, patient, strong-willed, son with a magnetic personality. You who taught me how to love fearlessly, laugh until I can't breathe, and fight with all my might.

To Austin, my red-headed techie, inquisitive, problem-solving, tenacious, forgiving, loving son with a heart so big his chest can hardly contain it. You make me think outside of the box and embrace my uniqueness. Your endless hugs and questions warm my heart and test my patience. You are a perfect balance.

To Asher, my strong-willed, confident, informative, nurturing, artistic, musical, riddling, architect. You challenge me to continue to learn and grow, to change my perspective, and find joy in singing and dancing. You are my favorite dance partner and singer.

Table of Contents

PREFACE 7

CHANGE OF PLANS 11

YOU DIDN'T DO ANYTHING WRONG… 26

PERSPECTIVE CHANGES EVERYTHING 26

YOU CAN'T CONTROL EVERYTHING! (I'VE TRIED IT'S EXHAUSTING, AND IT DOESN'T WORK!) 33

DO IT SCARED 42

MISTAKES WILL BE MADE… 49

HELP PLEASE! 49

STRUGGLE BUS= 58

SPED PARENT LIFE 58

BOSS UP! 64

TAKE CARE 72

ENJOY THE MOMENTS 79

BUT I LOVE IT HERE! 84

THE WORLD NEEDS MORE SCARLETS 90

LOVE IS WAITING 95

DREAM A NEW DREAM 102

MY DREAM 109

"Life would be tragic if it weren't funny"

-Stephan Hawking

(Diagnosed with Amyotrophic Lateral Sclerosis (ALS))

Preface

Before you put this book down, this is not another sob story about how my life is soooooo hard, I'm on the struggle bus and I don't know how I'm going to endure such a challenging life! I have yet to finish one of those books. I have enough issues, reading about someone else who has the same issues or worse and not being able to cope will not:

- make me feel any better about my current or future situation.
- help me change my current or future situation.
- give me hope that I can endure and that there is light and joy somewhere.
- change my perspective so I can shift my thinking and how I view my child and situation.

BUT WHAT IT WILL DO:

- Make me feel like I'm stuck, and nothing will ever get better. I will see myself in this person and see that they are losing a losing battle.

WHO WANTS TO READ THAT?!?!?!!?

Not me! I already have enough going on in my reality. I don't need to read about anyone else's struggles and how they are barely making it.

SOOOOOOOOOOOO...

The goal of this book is to uplift and encourage you. To let you know that you are not alone. Some of the things you have been thinking about, I have thought about them too and so have many others.

I'm writing this book because <u>I NEED THIS BOOK</u>! I need some encouragement. I need to laugh about this crazy life I'm living. I need to know that I'm not alone… that I'm not crazy (Well maybe a little bit). You must be a little crazy to get through this life without losing it completely. I need to know that it's okay for me to feel all the things I'm feeling at any given time.

So I am writing this book to allow you to feel "normal" while embracing the fact that there is nothing normal about you and your life. Or at least feel as though you are not alone…there is someone out here just as crazy and dysfunctional as you! Hopefully, reading this book will help you release some heaviness and anxiety. And you will feel encouraged and inspired. I hope that reading this book will change your perspective of your life, child, and future.

THEN…

you will be able to embrace this super amazing, challenging, exhausting, complicated, no manual we are winging it, uncomfortable, unpredictable, laugh until you pee on yourself (just a little bit), empowering, satisfying life we have!

I'm going to be okay!

You're going to be okay!

Our children are going to be okay!

Everything will be BETTER than okay!

"I'm officially disabled, but I'm truly enabled because of my lack of limbs. My unique challenges have opened up unique opportunities to reach so many in need."

–Nick Vujicic

(Born with extremely rare congenital condition called **Tetra-amelia syndrome**)

Chapter 1

Change of Plans

I thought about it again today. Sometimes it's a fleeting thought when I feel overwhelmed and other times, I plan out the whole scenario. How will I do it? What will happen to my boys? I convince myself they will be better off without me. That someone will do a better job. Someone else won't yell as much. They will have more patience. They will plan more and think further ahead. They will spend more time researching. They will never forget to do therapy plans at home. They will put Andrew in his stander twice a day. They will make sure they remember to laugh, play and enjoy life with the boys. Anybody will be better than me.

And then Austin walks into the garage and taps on the window. He asks if I'm okay with love and concern in his eyes as tears stream down my face. "Do you need a hug, Mommy?" he asks. And then I remember they are my gifts handpicked for me. I have a purpose to fulfill as their mom. I'm chosen for them, and they for me. I am their terribly flawed mother, and my boys wouldn't have it any other way.

I knew I was pregnant before anyone else. I'm such a "Fertile Myrtle." We were trying, but I didn't think it would happen so quickly. I hadn't taken a pregnancy test yet, there was just a knowing inside of me that I was pregnant. It was too early to start taking pregnancy tests or make an appointment with my OBGYN, but I knew. His presence was powerful even at conception.

It turns out I was right! I knew for sure at four weeks, and a physician confirmed it. I was pregnant! I could barely catch my breath. I was so ecstatic! I had been waiting for the majority of my adult life for this moment. "First comes love, then comes marriage, then comes the baby in the baby carriage!" That's when the dreaming began. This was when he became the brilliant, god-fearing, and loving, world changer. He was the tall, handsome, athletic, well-mannered son who loved his mama and made her proud. As I type this, I'm chuckling because all of my dreams have come true even more than I could have imagined, just not how ***I*** imagined. Why does everything have to be so colorful and eventful? Why can't life just stick to the blueprint you have drawn out so perfectly? I can prepare for that! I can handle that! The keyword here is **"I."**

I could have handled my perfectly dreamed-up child on my own, but I would have missed out on all that God had in store for us if God had stuck to my plan. God gave me Andrew's name before I even knew his gender. Andrew Jeremiah is a warrior whom God will raise up. His namesake scripture is Jeremiah 29:10-11. I love The Message version of this scripture:

> **"...I'll show up and take care of you as I promised and bring you back home. I know what I'm doing. I have it all planned out-plans to take care of you, not abandon you, plans to give you the future you hope for."**

Listen, Honey; this tells me I need to take my plans, tear them up, soak them in kerosene, light a match, set them ablaze, and ***take several seats***! If it was only that easy for me and this beautiful brain God gave me!

I am an educator, A.K.A. control freak! No shade to any of my educators out there, but ya'll know how it is. I must have everything planned to the t! My diet, my supplements, my midwife, my obstetrician, my birth plan, my birth music, and, of course, my wardrobe. I had Plan A, B, C, D, and D-squared. I read all the books about pregnancy and what to expect. I always feel more in control when I know what to expect. God and I have this conversation regularly. God says, "Trust me." I say, "I do, but can you tell me where I'm going, who's going to be there, what am I going to be doing. How do I need to prepare? what will the outcome be, and do I need to buy a new pair of shoes for this?" Yes, that's me all day long. So, I educated myself on what to expect to be prepared for all scenarios, at least that's what I thought.

Okay, enough about me and my craziness. Let me talk about this amazing little boy that was being knitted together in my womb and giving me the excuse to eat cookies whenever I wanted, because no one ever asked the pregnant lady how many she had!

Since we wanted to discover the baby's gender at birth, I began calling this amazing little being "Fruit" based on the scripture that says, "*The fruit of your womb will be blessed.*" (Duet.28:4) I started talking and reading to Fruit. I would play all types of music and sing. We sang and danced daily. I ate all the "right" foods to help my little fruit grow healthy and strong. Okay, 80% of the time I ate all the "right" foods. But, Friend, those cookies and fries were calling me! I'm not even going to try to blame my little "Fruit." I wanted all the cookies with a side of fries!

The amount of research I did was insane. But it was also my way of keeping myself sane. This was uncharted territory for me, so I felt that I could handle all things pregnancy if I was overly informed. It was my way of staying in control of the situation. Not knowing it was all in vain. I had no control at all.

In addition to being an educator, I'm super "granola", meaning I prefer the natural approach to all things. I was healthy and believed that my body could give birth without interventions such as induction or epidurals. So, after consulting with Andrew's father, my husband at the time, my midwife, and my obstetrician, I decided to have a home birth. Everyone thought I was crazy, especially since this was my first child. But I didn't care. It felt right. Everything about the pregnancy felt right. I had a great pregnancy. All of the ultrasounds we had zero red flags, and no abnormalities. My convictions and faith were strong about my decision.

Change of Plans

I know I read "Supernatural Childbirth" by Jackie Mize at least three times. Some parts are etched in my mind and heart forever. "Supernatural Childbirth" is a book written by the missionary Terry Mize's wife. She believed in God for quick and painless childbirths. She based her requests on scriptures from God's word, revelation she was shown, and in faith that God would grant her request, not asking out of fear. God granted her requests. Many women have testified that after reading this book and making the same requests in faith, not fear, God granted their requests also. So, my morning and evening time with God was spent meditating on those scriptures, making my requests, and preparing myself mentally and spiritually for what was to come. I had no idea what was to come, but God did, and this preparation and intimate time with Him gave me the strength and fortitude I needed to withstand what I would face at birth and after.

The Dream

Honestly, I hadn't focused on having a healthy child. Of course, I wanted a healthy child. Isn't that what every mom wants? I guess I thought I was doing all the right things regarding health. Therefore, I didn't focus my prayers and dreams on how long his umbilical cord would be or that he wouldn't experience hypoxia and have his basal ganglia damaged in childbirth, leading to cerebral palsy. It was a given, right? It all falls under the umbrella of "healthy baby". Everything was going to be okay right? Although I knew what could happen, I didn't think to pray, "Oh God, please don't let my child have cerebral palsy or any other disability." Maybe, I didn't see it as a huge concern because I work with students with different abilities daily, and I had a different perspective. Perhaps it was because I knew that my mom had been praying for her grandchildren for over a decade, so surely her prayers would be answered. Or maybe, it wouldn't have mattered anyway because God had Andrew's life already planned before his conception. (Jeremiah 29:11)

My dreams for him were that he would love God more than anything. He would have a personal, authentic relationship with God early in life and fulfill his purpose and destiny while on Earth. I hoped that he would be intelligent.

Dream Changer

I hoped that he would be athletic and strong. I hoped that he would be brave and stand up for what was right. Finally, I hoped that he would bring honor to our family. I had no idea that all of my dreams would come true, just not how I expected.

Do I feel guilty for not praying and dreaming that I would have a healthy son and be okay with whatever else happened? **Yes! Absolutely!** Do I second guess my decision to have my son at home instead of a hospital? **Yes! Absolutely!** Do I blame myself for all of it? **Yes! Absolutely!** Do I often wonder what life would be like if I had chosen differently and Andrew was a "typical boy"? **Yes! Absolutely!** Am I ashamed that I wonder about those things? **Yes! Absolutely!** The terribly flawed human that I am sometimes wonders about these things. Is that okay?

Yes! Absolutely!

The Birth

Fruit and I developed a special bond while being my every growing fanny pack for thirty-six and a half weeks. I read to him, put headphones on my stomach and played classical music, I sang to him and prayed over him. My favorite was singing to him. To this day, he loves music. I sang all the time. Music for me was and still is like air. I sing through trials and victories. It is my therapy. When I'm happy or sad there is always a song in my heart. While pregnant, I sang on the praise team at my church. My heart was always in a position of praise and worship throughout the pregnancy. Little did know praise and worship would carry Fruit and I through the most challenging times of our lives...when we both would need to just **breathe.**

Change of Plans

The birth was beautiful. I'm not kidding. I know you're probably thinking, "Ma'am, I don't know how you can say that any part of childbirth could be beautiful. You are truly trippin'!" I am that weird person who feels great pleasure and fulfillment in working hard for something and even feeling a certain amount of pain to get a priceless reward. It was the hardest and most satisfying thing I had ever done in my life. I would do it again in a heartbeat to have my "Three Wisemen" (that's what I sometimes call my sons).

The labor progressed normally. His heart rate was normal, he was still very active, and he was ready to come out. I was eight centimeters dilated and could get into the tub, the wonderful, glorious tub filled with warm water. It was a natural epidural. I relaxed more through the contractions, and I continued to dilate quickly. I remember having the urge to push when I got in the water. This overwhelming urgency had nothing to do with pain or the birthing process. My inner counsel told me Andrew needed to come quickly, and I had to make sure that happened. I pushed hard and strong, and he was out in 15 minutes.

I UNDERSTOOD THE ASSIGNMENT!

Unbeknownst to me, Andrew came out placenta and all. I picked him up and put him on my chest. My midwife allowed his father to cut the umbilical cord. Andrew was so quiet and tiny, and he had a head full of curly black hair. "Andrew! My beautiful Andrew Jeremiah!" I was crying tears of joy. Little did I know that they would be tears of sorrow, fear, and terror in seconds.

My rejoicing over the new addition to our family was interrupted by my midwife's calm and gentle voice. **"Jamila, I need you to let me take a look at Andrew."** I was confused and then looked at his skin. I was an awful shade of gray and he was so quiet. He hadn't made a sound, not one move. My midwife took him and laid him on the floor, padded with towels to check his vitals. She couldn't find a heartbeat, he wasn't breathing…no signs of life.

He was gone...

My midwife began CPR immediately. I looked at my mom, who was holding the camera. Her eyes filled with tears, and her heart was breaking. She dropped the camera and fell to her knees, calling out to God on Andrew's behalf. I sat in the tub and let out a groan I can still hear and feel in the pit of my stomach now. I didn't have any words, but I knew God could listen to my heart.

My midwife's assistant called 911, and my midwife continued CPR. I hung over the side of the bathtub, groaning and sobbing, as I watched my son's tiny lifeless body. Words?!?! I needed words! Finally! I screamed,

"God! Breathe your breath of life into Andrew! He will live and not die and declare the works of the Lord!"

At that moment, Andrew's little chest began to rise and fall. ***"I've got a heartbeat!"*** That was the first of many miracles.

The EMS arrived minutes later, took over with oxygen, and checked his vitals. He was alive! My baby was back! They took him away so quickly I didn't have a chance to kiss him goodbye and let him know I love him. I wanted to let him know it would be okay and Mommy's coming. I wanted him to know he wasn't alone, Mommy's here…

As the ambulance whisked away my firstborn son, I was still in the tub. I was in a state of shock. The moments after the ambulance took Andrew away were gut-wrenching. All I felt was the emptiness of my womb and my arms.

All I felt was the emptiness of my womb and my arms.

Change of Plans

The picture I painted in my dreams of a beautiful birth and a perfect baby boy, my Andrew Jeremiah, was gone instantly.

- What did I do?
- What have I done to deserve this?
- What did I do that was so terrible to warrant such a thing to happen to my child?

I have loved God for as long as I can remember and always tried to do what was right.

- ✓ I used my gift of singing for His Glory every Sunday morning and Wednesday night at church.
- ✓ I waited to have children until I got married.

I did what I thought I was supposed to do.

- ✓ I did my research.
- ✓ I ate well and exercised.
- ✓ I got my rest.

What did I miss? What did I do wrong? I teach children with special needs. I pay it forward.

Why is this happening to me?

When I screamed, "MY BABY!" It encompassed all of those questions. All I wanted was my baby. The one that I prepared for and dreamed of almost nightly. I wanted the Andrew Jeremiah God promised me!

As I laid on the bed, wet, naked, bleeding, and numb; I kept saying, "My baby, my baby, I have to go with my baby." But I couldn't go anywhere. I had to get cleaned up and pee.

Ya'll, I wanted to slap my midwife! I wanted to make sure she never tasted anything again! She kept telling me I could not leave until I peed! Why?!?! I didn't have to pee! I didn't want to pee! I wanted to be with my Andrew, my baby!

Much to my chagrin, I finally peed. Only God knew how hard and painful peeing was after birth. MERCY! Trying to get your body to do what your mind is telling it to before it is ready is an awesome feat! I barely felt the pain because I was numb from the inside out. My heart was in an ambulance, and I needed to be with my baby.

My midwife got me onto the bed. My mom was on the floor in a ball, crying, praying, and grieving. Andrew's father went with him in the ambulance. I lay on the bed, still wet and cold, as my midwife examined me. She showed me the placenta and the tiny umbilical cord attached. I had no idea how significant this would be later. I tried to pay attention to what she was saying, but all I could hear was the silence that came from Andrew. It was deafening. He never made a single sound.

As I lay there, half-naked and still bleeding, I began screaming, "I want my baby! Take me to my baby!" I was on the brink of hysteria. My mother pulled herself up from the floor, plopped on the bed, looked me in the eyes, and said, "Stop it! Stop it right now! We don't have time for this! Get yourself together!"

I didn't shed a tear for months after that moment. I wish she would've let me cry and feel everything I was feeling, just for a few more minutes. I died that day. The moment he was born, I died. My life was no longer about me. It was completely taken over when I became Andrew's mother. I didn't matter anymore. I didn't get to feel anything anymore. I had to "fix" Andrew.

Against my midwife's advice, I took a shower, put on some clothes, and padded myself as well as I could. My mom drove me to the hospital, and the hospital staff met me with a wheelchair. They took me to him. He was so tiny. All he had on was a diaper, no blanket, no little sleeper, just wires and machines all around. I needed to hold him and feed him on my breast. I knew he had to be hungry. He was shaking, so I pulled out a blanket for him, and the nurse handed him to me. He is still shaking. The nurse said they thought Andrew was having seizures, that was the reason he was shaking. The moment I took him in my arms, I could breathe again. I didn't even know I was holding my breath. He looked up at me, and I knew he would be okay. I also knew things would never be the same.

The NICU

Andrew never nursed. We tried and tried that night, but he was not strong enough. He made some movements, but his muscles would not listen to his brain. They still won't listen.

So, we spent 31 days in the PNICU. They poked and prodded my baby every 2-3 hours. How could he rest and heal? I remember hearing the results of his first MRI. Everything at this time was just speculation because the human body is so amazing and has proven to be self-heal over time. The pediatric neurologist showed us the images. This was all foreign to me. Although I was a special education teacher, I didn't know the neurological science behind each disability.

Andrew's brain was without oxygen for 15-20 minutes while passing through the birth canal. He was without oxygen because he took the placenta with him as he moved through the birth canal. His umbilical cord was not even a foot long and was the circumference of my index finger. This was his tiny lifeline all this time. It went undetected during each ultrasound. They told us everything was fine. "He's just a little small," the doctor said.

Of course, we know lack of oxygen can damage the brain. The part of Andrew's brain that was affected due to hypoxia was the basal ganglia, which controls muscle tone and movement. This explained why he wasn't nursing. Everything else seemed fine. All babies are floppy and weak when they are born. So, his body felt "normal." His movement felt "normal."

My faith is all I had to hold on to when we were in the PICU. I made signs for his bed with scriptures. I made an audio of me talking and singing to Andrew. I quoted healing scriptures and wrote a song for him. "Lord, I thank you for healing Andrew. Lord, I thank you for healing Andrew, for there's nothing too hard for You. You are whole, spirit, mind, body, and soul. You are whole, spirit, mind, body, and soul. For there's nothing too hard for God." I left this recording of me in his little crib every time they made me go to take a shower and eat. I didn't want him to think I was leaving him or be scared because he didn't hear mommy. His presence was my air now. Every time I left him, I held my breath until I held him again. I needed to protect him and be with him for both of us to be okay.

Our time in the PICU was hard. Especially in the first few days. Infants were fighting for their lives and losing the fight. I remember the first time I came back from taking a shower and getting something to eat. Andrew was moved to a different area where another baby had just been. I felt fear in my stomach that I had never experienced before. I was afraid because I didn't see him for a moment, and thought, "What has happened to him? Is he gone again, for good this time?" When I spotted him, I rushed over and scooped him up in my arms and wept. I wept because I was so thankful that he was still alive. I cried for the child who was now gone and the mother who lost her child. I rocked and wept until I had no more tears. I remember waking up to the nurse gently taking Andrew from my arms for his routine checks.

After a few more days, Andrew was stable enough to be moved to the NICU. This allowed us to have our little corner and more privacy. The days had become a blur. I was still recovering from childbirth, but I wasn't going anywhere without my baby! The doctors, nurses, and therapists would come in and out of his little space all day and night. They relentlessly poked and prodded him. I wanted to make sure that I was there for every encounter to make sure the staff knew Andrew had a mother who loves him and cares about what happens to him. It was exhausting, but they needed to know that Andrew's mother didn't blindly trust them and wouldn't allow them to do whatever they wanted because he was a helpless infant. He was my baby boy.

Change of Plans

After being in our corner for a few more days, the doctors and nurses began to talk to me about Andrew getting a G-tube put in. A G-tube is a surgically placed device used to give direct access to your child's stomach for supplemental feeding, hydration, or medication. Umm, no thank you! I know that a G-tube could be life-saving for many children with various needs. However, I knew that Andrew would be able to eat by mouth he just needed more time.

Needless to say, I declined the G-tube and told the doctors that taking care of Andrew was now my full-time job. I let them know that Andrew and I would stay in the NICU as long as we needed to in order for him to eat by mouth. I said what I said.

The next day, the doctors put in an order for Andrew and me to have our own room. The room was set up like a bedroom. No monitors beeping and no other families a few feet away. We had a door and our own bathroom! The only thing Andrew needed to do was eat on his own. He had to take in two ounces of milk by mouth consistently over 24 hours and he would be able to come home. He also needed to not lose any weight. It has been proven repeatedly that patients who are stable heal more quickly at home. They can rest and thrive when they are comfortable and at home.

Andrew and I were moved in to this little "bedroom". My mom and I set it up to give it a warm home feel. No bright lights, essential oils diffusing, television playing low in the background during the day, and most importantly, we prayed. We asked God to let this stay in the room be brief so Andrew could finally come home.

He ate well during his scheduled feeding time during the day! Night fell and I couldn't sleep at all. I would just watch him sleep. He was so peaceful. No one came in to bother us every two hours. He could finally rest and that is just what he did. He slept, for five hours straight and when he woke up he was hungry and ready to eat! He ate the most he had ever eaten! My baby was tired! He needed rest and to feel hunger!

We were discharged the following day! A nurse would come to visit daily for the first month, just to make sure he was still eating, growing, and thriving. Every time she came, he had made improvements!

We were finally home! I had no idea what life was going to be like. At this point I had no idea how much the damage to Andrew's brain would affect his daily functioning or intelligence. What I did know is God had his hand on Andrew's life from the beginning. God chose to allow Andrew to come back to us. I know God has a plan and purpose for Andrew. I know that I am Andrew's mother, and I am honored. I know that this will be a journey through uncharted territory, but we will get through it. I don't know how, but I know we will.

"I do not have a disability; I have a gift! Others may see it as a disability, but I see it as a challenge. This challenge is a gift because I have to become stronger to get around it, and smarter to figure out how to use it; others should be so lucky."

— Shane E. Bryan (diagnosed with Dystonia)

Chapter 2

You Didn't Do Anything Wrong... Perspective Changes Everything

You Didn't Do Anything Wrong...

I honestly don't know how often I have asked God what I did wrong. I must have done something wrong. I second-guessed every decision I made concerning the pregnancy and the birth. I was so adamant about having a home birth. Would he have been born alive if I had him at the hospital? Did I choose the wrong doctor? Maybe if I had chosen a different doctor, he would have noticed something wasn't right with the umbilical cord. I am ashamed to share that I thought Andrew's diagnosis was a punishment. When I think about it, sounds so arrogant Like this all has something to do with me. I must have done something terrible to have something like this happen to my child. I wondered if my son's condition was a punishment or a curse for something I did wrong in my past. Maybe, I didn't pray or read the Bible enough. I didn't pray the proper prayer, eat the right foods, or take enough vitamins.

The truth of the matter is, **I DIDN'T DO ANYTHING WRONG, AND NEITHER DID YOU!** There is nothing that you or I did to cause anything to happen to your child. Can I explain why it happened? No. I wish I could. I would love to know the why and the purpose of it all, but I may never know, and I can't dwell on that. What I also can't do is punish myself or blame myself for my child's condition. Whom does that help? NO ONE! Continuing to blame yourself will be your fault and will hurt your child. So, stop!

Decide today that you will stop beating yourself up for something that isn't your fault, even if an accident happened and caused harm. It was an accident; it was not intentional. At some point, you must forgive yourself to be healthy and present for your child. We can't change what happened, but we can change how we approach the future. Oh, and guess what? You are going to do many things wrong throughout your child's life. You are not perfect and THANK GOD you don't have to be. So, stop dwelling on how things started and whether or not you did something wrong. You can't go back there, but you can move forward and wholeheartedly do your best to provide your child with the best life possible, mistakes and all.

"No doubt about it: Children are a gift from the Lord; the fruit of the womb is a divine reward." Psalm 127:3 (Common English Bible)

This verse says it all, but to be clear one more time for the people in the back!

YOUR CHILD IS NOT A PUNISHMENT OR A CURSE! YOUR CHILD IS A BLESSING, AND A REWARD.

Don't worry, you are not alone. When thinking about what you did wrong.

Look, bad things are going to happen, Period! That is just how life is set up. God does not give his children a magic blanket that covers and protects them from bad things happening, the wrong people or sad situations. So, stop expecting life to be perfect and trouble-free.

When awful things happen, our perspective is the key. The proper perspective will turn what seems to be an awful "how will I ever make it through this, why is this happening to me, I am a good person and always help other people, and I'm going to die or at least never get out of bed because the world is awful, and I'm the only person on the planet who has had awful things happen to me" moment into a blessing. You have an opportunity to experience a display of God's all-encompassing presence and protection.

SNAPSHOT OF LIFE WITH ANDREW:

You Didn't Do Anything Wrong...

It's 6:40 a.m. on a Wednesday. We must leave the house in 5 minutes to ensure that we make it to school on time. Andrew decides that he has a pressing question that can't wait until we get in the van. He must ask his question at this very moment. So I have to stop what I am doing and wait for him to ask me about his 5th grade graduation for the third time this morning. His brothers have already asked me a million questions already this morning, so I can't deny Andrew the opportunity. The clock is ticking! He already knows the answer to the question he is asking! Lord, my patience and my nerves! Because it is important to him and me that he is heard. I wait, listen, and answer him. Are we late? Yes! Is it worth it? ABSOLUTELY! Okay, we can look at this as an inconvenience (punishment) or a gift.

- **Punishment**: We will be late for the millionth time because it takes so long for Andrew to express himself.

- **GIFT**: My son can and wants to communicate with me! My son is intelligent enough to read and use a communication device to organize words and phrases to express himself. He is tenacious enough not to give up until you clearly understand what he is saying. (A large percentage of verbal children his age cannot do that.)

Perspective is everything!! Perspective can change the trajectory of your moments, days, and life.

I remember wanting to find a school for Andrew that would allow him to be in the general education setting. Andrew was too bright to be limited to spending his entire day in a special education classroom just because he was in a wheelchair and used a communication device.

Now let's be real, when in those awful "how will I ever make it through this why is this happening to me I am a good person, and always help other people, I'm going to die or at least never get out of bed because the world is awful, and I'm clearly the only person on the planet who has very bad things happen to me." moments you can't see anything but the situation. We must find a way not to fall apart every time something happens, big or small. I used to be that person. It wasn't very good, and I might be slightly dramatic, so that didn't help either. Honestly, anything that would deviate from the plan that I had in my head for the day or my life would lead to these "adult tantrums." It was exhausting, non-productive, sometimes debilitating, and downright uncalled for. Sometimes I would lose a whole day because I couldn't get past Andrew being denied for some equipment or services. I would fall apart if Andrew pooped in the tub before bed and threw our entire nighttime routine off. Also, because he pooped in the tub. I don't care how much poop I clean up at home or school, poop is gross, and I don't like cleaning it up.

However, I began to find the blessings. First, I had to see God's presence and protection in every situation because it was there, even with the poop in the tub. Now you may have to squinch your eyes, tilt your head to the left, hold your mouth in the "selfie duck lip" pose, put your hands in the prayer position while standing on one foot and counting backward from 10. Still, if you focus on finding the blessing more than dwelling on the problem, you will find it.

I could've focused on the poop. I could have cried, ranted and raved, locked myself in the room for an hour, and obsessed over how awful my life was. Other parents don't have to clean poop out of the tub (this has happened for maybe 15 minutes, but I told you I was dramatic, so that's where the hour came from). Or I can focus on the fact that Andrew can poop without any assistance. He doesn't get constipated or take medication daily to poop! I don't have to give him rectal massages to help him poop! Ummmm, can we say blessing! How many parents would love to say, "Yeah, so my kid pooped in the tub last night?"

And guess what else, you are not alone. I know it feels that way. The enemy wants you to feel like you and your child are on an island surrounded by judgment, opinions, failures, hurt, and fear. But the truth is, according to the National Library of Medicine, there are 11.2 million children with special needs in the United States. One in five households care for a child with special needs. So, you are definitely not alone. You could walk a few houses down in your neighborhood and encounter someone caring for a child with different abilities. I know you feel lonely, and your situation seems unique. But honestly, when you look at it from the perspective of, I'm not the only one going through this, you realize millions of people are in similar situations or have the same experiences. All of these people can't be horrible and are being punished for all of their bad choices and decisions. When you change your perspective, you begin to open up a bit to the idea that maybe things will be okay. Will it be different than what you hoped and dreamed? YES! But it WILL be okay. So often, when we know and understand that others are walking the same path, we take on the mentality, "If they can do it, so can I!" It is encouraging to know that it is possible to parent a child with special needs, successfully get them through the public school system, and help them live extraordinary lives without losing your mind and enjoying life along the way. Perspective is a game-changer when you have a complete dream change.

As a disabled man, let my life be a reflection of the endless amount of ability that exists in each and every one of us.

-Robert M. Hensel

(Born with Spina Bifida)

Chapter 3

You Can't Control Everything! (I've tried it's exhausting, and it doesn't work!)

I put a hole in the wall once. Yes, an actual hole. I was angry, frustrated, overwhelmed, and feeling incompetent. I know you must be reading this asking yourself, "Did she actually punch a hole in the wall?" Okay, so before ya'll start some crazy rumor about me, I did not punch a hole in the wall. First, that is not how I react when angry, frustrated, overwhelmed, or having feelings of incompetence. We all know violence is not the answer. Secondly, I'm a delicate flower and would never be able to punch a hole in a wall. Well, maybe if you messed with one of my boys, I digress.

Okay, back to the hole in the wall. I put a hole in the wall, with Andrew's new wheelchair. It is a fantastic chair with bells and whistles, including a sit-to-stand feature. Just when I had finally mastered his old chair. I could whip that bad boy around and in and out of places with no problem. Andrew was a pro as well. We all know children eventually outgrow their equipment, and we have to replace it and start from scratch.

This new chair is an adult chair and totally different from Andrew's old chair. His old pediatric chair had a front-wheel drive so that it could make tight turns and maneuver through the house easily. Well, this new chair is larger, has arear-wheel drive, turns like a Mack truck, and we haven't made it through the house yet without taking out a wall or piece of furniture.

Getting into our house through the garage is tricky. We have a ramp inside the garage, and the landing that Andrew has to turn on to enter the house is just big enough for him to turn and straighten up. Being the helpful, slightly overbearing mother who can't stand watching her son struggle, I tried to intervene. Now ordinarily, I would fight the "Takeover Spirit" and let him figure it out on his own or until he asks for help. But this was his second time driving, so I felt it was okay to jump in. Nope! That was not a good idea. I should've let him figure it out. But no, I had to put my cape on, be "Super Mom," and try to save the day.

Welp! Instead of saving the day, I redecorated the foyer with a new hole in the wall. I don't want you to think this was just a little dent or quarter size hole in the wall. This whole required several YouTube video tutorials on how to repair sheetrock and a consult from my dad. Ultimately resulting in me buying a metal kickplate to cover up the huge gaping hole in our foyer. No matter how many tutorials I watched this mama was not going to patch sheetrock.

I didn't have it all figured out. I still don't have Andrew's chair figured out. I have no idea how middle school would work, and he was starting in 3 weeks! I just threw up in my mouth a little bit, but it will be okay. I didn't know his teachers or his adult support person (who will be with him more than me throughout the day). I don't know what bus he would be riding, and I still haven't figured out what he will do after school. This had never been an issue before because he had always been with me. He would usually come to my class after school.

It's okay not to know what's next, but it drives me crazy! As I said earlier, God is not through with me yet when it comes to me wanting to know everything so I can plan for it. As I am typing this, I still get an awful feeling in my stomach thinking about Andrew going to middle school. **MIDDLE SCHOOL!** I work in the public school system, which made me even more nervous about the whole situation. I know way too much!

For twelve years, Andrew had been by my side or at least within walking distance of me. Being a divorcee and single mother, I have been blessed to be with all my boys throughout their educational careers. So, the thought of Andrew not being under my vigilant watchful eye was terrifying, unnerving, frightening, horrifying, and paralyzing!

WARNING!!!! WHAT YOU ARE ABOUT TO READ IS VERY DRAMATIC.

You are already 3 chapters in so this shouldn't be surprising. No matter how dramatic I sound, this is how I felt in my heart and spirit. I had gone over so many possible scenarios in my head of things that could happen to Andrew. I have had literal movies play out in my head with theme music! Of course, it doesn't help that I'm a very visual person, and I dream in color!

Oh, the list I had of what could go wrong with Andrew in Middle School…

The List:

- Andrew will get bullied, and no one would want to be his friend.

- Andrew's paraprofessional will neglect him and not help him at school. They won't feed, dry, or help him with his schoolwork. Instead, they will leave him to sit and fend for himself.

- Andrew will be totally and completely unhappy, and will be mistreated, he won't want to go to school, and I won't be able to do anything about it because I have to work being that I'm a single mom of three! (Gasping for breath… try reading all that in one breath) that is exactly how I wrote it! I was holding my breath while typing this one. That's how anxious I was about this particular bullet point.

- Andrew's teacher will not see him or want to help him. Instead, they will see him as just another nonverbal kid in a wheelchair.

- Andrew's teacher will recommend that he be placed in a self-contained classroom. That would change the trajectory of his school career.

- Andrew will not perform at the level that he is performing now because of the lack of support.

You Can't Control Everything!

I could dedicate a whole chapter to the list that I had in my head of all the things that could go wrong with Andrew going to middle school.

The unknown is terrifying and ignites the imagination, causing you to worry, second guess your decisions, and lock your child in a room to protect them forever. It is okay to feel all of these feelings. As you have read, you are not alone.

You have the opportunity to either negatively spiral out of control or find the something positive. You either make a list of all the things that can go wrong or list all the things that can go right. I know it's easier said than done, **but it is a choice**. It is something that I have to choose. I have to choose to be positive. I have to choose to see the positive in circumstances and situations that appear negative. The alternative is a sleep-deprived, worried, anxious, and horrible mother. If I didn't make peace with the fact that I wasn't going to know what will happen in middle school. I don't know his teachers and how they really felt about having him in their class.

My imagination is vivid and colorful. The scenarios that came to mind are in retrospect, outlandish and even absurd, but seemed very real and possible at that moment. When I go back and read my journal entries, they remind me it will be okay. It's like giving myself a pep talk. "I know this seems impossible, but do you remember when you thought Andrew communicating using a device so others could understand him, so you wouldn't always have to be his personal interpreter was impossible? Clearly it wasn't impossible. It was hard and you had to be patient, but he is doing it! So, if you could get through that, surely you can get through this." I need to read these entries to pull me off a ledge sometimes. It helps me put things into perspective, calms my fears, and all the "what ifs." I can refocus and remember who is in control.

There are so many unknown things! There are so many things I can't control. Am I freaking out? Absolutely! This is why I keep a journal. When I have my freak-out moments about unexpected or uncontrollable things, and I have no idea what I will do, I get my journal. I don't write in my journal every night. I know I should, but the way my life is set up, sleep is more therapeutic most nights. I do take the time to write about the hard times, and then I go back and write about how God helped me through those times and how things worked out. Never how I planned or expected them to, but it is incredible how it is always better than I imagined. Eventually, you see how you needed everything you went through to get you to where you are right now and to strengthen you for what is to come.

"Let go and trust." It sounds so easy, right? I have lost count of the number of times I have heard "Read Psalms 91 to Andrew 3 times a day. Pray this prayer and that prayer. You have to just trust God, Andrew will be fine." These statements all come from sincere and good intentioned people. However, it is still coming from someone who did not carry Andrew for nine months only to have him swept away in an ambulance shortly after the first time you held him in your arms. It's coming from people who never spent a night in a PICU surrounded by ailing infants dying daily. People who have never experienced the heart-altering news that your child in which you have so many hopes and dreams will never be the child you dreamed of. It comes from people who have never spent a day, let alone 21 days, in the PICU/NICU. These people haven't endured watching a child wheeled away for the 9th surgery in their five-year-old life. Sometimes it's easier to trust God when you don't have to watch one of your most precious gifts go through hell daily.

It is not easy to trust and let go when you have invested so much prayer, time, energy, resources, and life into someone you love more than yourself. You want to hold on to them and protect them. You believe you are the only one who can love them and care for them properly. How dare anyone tell you to "Let go and trust"!

- ✓ They don't know your child like you do.
- ✓ They could never love your child like you do.
- ✓ Anyone could easily mistreat your child, and you would never know about it until it's too late.

The list goes on and on.

Fear is talking. This is fear manipulating your emotions to make you believe that everything is dangerous, and you are the only person who can love and care for your child. Once again, **FEAR IS A LIAR!** Yes, there are bad people in the world. Andrew will inevitably encounter some bad people in life. But honestly, most people are good and want to do their best to do right by Andrew. Do they make mistakes? Heck yeah! Shoot, I make mistakes all the time! Does that mean I should let fear paralyze me?

For years I agonized about Andrew growing up and being away from me once he reached the 6th grade. I told you that I am overly dramatic and have shared the awful things I imagined would happen to Andrew away from my watchful eye. I imagined him being laughed at and isolated from his peers, left all day in a soiled diaper, dropped and injured, mistreated and abused. I would play entire episodes in my head. It was pure torture, and I did this for years. After I divorced Andrew's father, I knew I would have to be a working single mother. I knew this meant I would have to allow someone else to care for Andrew so I could provide for our family. The Lord provided a way for me to be with my boys for their entire school career thus far. For two of those years, I was Andrew's teacher!

Andrew finished his 6th grade year! It was hard, stressful, exhausting, and extremely rewarding! Do you remember the list in Chapter 3? None of those things happened!

- ✓ Andrew was never bullied, and he made a ton of friends who are going to 7th grade with him.
- ✓ Andrew was blessed with the most amazing paraprofessional! She is truly an answered prayer. She was like his second mother. She would bake treats for him. She took a genuine interest in his likes and dislikes. They listened to music together. They belly laughed and had so much fun this school year! She is trying to figure out how she can continue with him next school year!

- ✓ Andrew was excited to go to school almost every day! He is human and a teenager so there were just days he did not want to get up. But 95% of the time he wanted to go to school!
- ✓ Andrew had the most amazing team of teachers. They wanted him to be successful and they went the extra mile to make sure he was included in classroom instruction and that assignments/tests aligned with his IEP.
- ✓ Not once did anyone on his team suggest that Andrew be in a self-contained classroom setting. Not once did anyone on his team say this placement is inappropriate for him. They were all supportive and eager to figure out how to help him succeed.
- ✓ Andrew finished the school year on the A/B Honor Roll!

It is scary. SPED(Special Education) parenting is terrifying! We can't let fear keep us from allowing our child to live and have new experiences. We must let go and trust. Okay, maybe not let go completely, that is just asking too much. But we must allow some space so that they will be able to grow. At some point, you must trust that God will take care of your child and allow people in their lives who will love them and care for them when they are not with you. If I would have held on to Andrew and not allowed myself to trust God, he wouldn't have had an amazing school year. And all the students, teachers, and staff would have been deprived of the wonderfulness that is Andrew!

"Disability is natural. We must stop believing that disabilities keep a person from doing something. Because that's not true . . . Having a disability doesn't stop me from doing anything."

-Benjamin Snow, Grade 8 diagnosed with Cerebral Palsy, Woodland Park, Colorado, in his essay "Attitudes About People with Disabilities"

Chapter 4

Do It Scared

It's okay to be scared. There are so many things that I'm afraid of when it comes to parenting and caring for Andrew. Is he happy? Does something hurt, and he isn't telling me? Did someone hurt him, and he doesn't know how to tell me or doesn't want to get the person in trouble? Does he want to walk, or is he okay with being in a wheelchair? Does he have friends, or are all the kids just pitying him? Will he ever have real friends and find love? Will he have a family? Will he live with me always? Does he want to live with me always? What happens at school when I'm not around? Is he learning? Am I doing enough, or do I make him sad? What does he want to be when he grows up?

The list goes on and on. I'm afraid I will never know the answers to these questions, and I will fail him. I'm worried I won't be able to protect him from this complex and cruel world. I'm afraid of stepping back and letting him grow up and become more independent. I'm afraid that no one will love him. I'm scared he will be mistreated. I'm afraid I won't live forever to make sure he is okay.

This life we live is terrifying and filled with unknowns, but we can't give up. Not on yourself. Not on your child.

There is purpose in every breath you take, every tear you cry, and every hurt you feel.

There is purpose in every mistake you think you made and every step you take backward. You are here, and your child is here for a divine purpose. It is not always clear. Let's be honest; it is almost always never clear. Most days, I feel like I'm shooting in the dark. Just throwing arrows and bullets at everything, trying to hit a bull's eye, only to walk toward the target and see all the arrows on the ground.

Some days I have adult tantrums. And you know what? That is okay, for like an hour. Well, not really an hour because I don't have the time or energy for that. But I allow myself to feel all the feelings because my feelings are valid, and they need to be expressed and felt. Then it is time to snap out of it! Giving up is not an option and nobody wants to come to my pity party. I use my time listening to uplifting music, watching motivational YouTube videos, calling a friend, playing with my little person, doing something we enjoy, and taking a nap. Everything is better after a nap!

I can remember one summer I was afraid to let Andrew go to summer camp at the YMCA with his brothers. Okay, let me back that up. I was scared even to call and ask if the summer camp would accept a nonverbal little boy in a wheelchair. I didn't do well with Andrew being rejected or not given a chance, and we got a lot of it. I took it personally, even though it wasn't personality was protocol. I wanted Andrew to be able to experience the same types of things his brothers did. I knew he didn't want to sit at home with me while his brothers were off at camp. So, I picked up the phone, took a deep breath, and called the Y. Much to my surprise, the program director was open to giving it a try! I felt like a kid asking for a cookie before dinner and being super surprised when my mom said, "yes". Remember, it's always a "no" until you ask.

Most of the time, the asking part is the hardest.

Now that he could go to summer camp with his brothers, I began to torture myself with all the unknown and the list of possible things that could happen while he was at camp for three hours right down the street from our home. I almost didn't take him. I almost convinced myself that this wasn't a good idea and he needed to stay home with me. That would have put my mind at ease, but it would've caused Andrew to miss out on a fantastic experience. It would also have not allowed those who worked with the camp and the children who attended the camp to experience Andrew's pure awesomeness. So, I reluctantly took him.

One little boy, in particular, took an interest in being Andrew's friend. He wrote him a note and asked the person with Andrew to give it to him. The message read, "Hi! My name is John. I think you are really cool. I would like to be your friend and have a playdate. Here's my mom's number ***-***-****. Have your mom call my mom. Love, John". When I read it, I couldn't hold back the tears. Fear is a liar and will keep you from all the beautiful experiences God has planned for you!

This letter sparked a friendship that has lasted for years. Not only did Andrew gain a friend, but I gained one as well. Amy is that friend who forces me to do things I wouldn't ordinarily do because I am that girly girl who likes to stay in her comfort zone. Well, all of that goes out the window when we get together!

This chick had me on a stripper pole and in the wilderness camping!

We will just talk about the camping trip and leave the stripper pole story for another time! Let me say it's not what you are thinking. I've been through some hard times, but God has kept us, and I have never had to turn to the pole to keep a roof over our heads. The Lord knows I would not have made any money. I couldn't even stay on the pole! I did have like a $50 moment but no rent money moves!

Okay, back to camping. Amy somehow convinced Andrew that all he wanted to do for his 10th birthday was go camping. They always plot stuff that drives me crazy or forces me out of my comfort zone. So, Andrew started asking me to go camping. Andrew is relentless when he gets an idea in his head! I have a tough time telling my boys no, especially when it will be a great experience and opportunity to make memories. Therefore, I agreed to a birthday camping trip.

Be afraid!

Be terrified!

DO IT ANYWAY!!!!

I had to admit we were having fun! We pitched the tents and cooked dinner over an open fire. The boys played and Andrew thought it was funny to sneak off and drive into the woods and scare the crap out of me. I would run and go get him and would find him laughing hysterically. Little bugger!

Everything was fine until the sun went down. There was a cat stalking me shortly after we started cooking. I couldn't get that cat to leave me alone. I was already nervous and anxious about sleeping outside in a tent and now I have a "cat stalker"! Amy and I got the boys into the tents and in their sleeping bags. All was well until I developed an overactive bladder. I know I went to the bathroom at least five times that night. The bathroom was like a half a mile away! Well, maybe not that far away but it was not a hop, skip, and a jump. I had to get my life together 5 different times in the middle of the night on this campground to go use the bathroom. Every time I said a little prayer and then I took off like Jason was coming after me with a chainsaw! I was booking it and every time I would look to the left and see "the cat stalker" It made me run even faster! I'm surprised I did have an accident on the way to the bathroom.

The next morning, Amy found Andrew and me in the van with the motor running and the heat blasting! Chile, that night was an adventure! Whenever you ask Andrew if he wants to go camping again, it is a hard "NO!" But at least we have the memories and the pictures. I didn't let fear or being uncomfortable keep us from finding out what I already knew; we don't like camping. Well, I am open to camping if a luxury RV is involved!

Be afraid. Sometimes you have just to do things afraid. You can be shaking in your boots but take a step anyway. Nine times out of 10, you will find that what you feared never happened, and what you could have never imagined happened. Like I said before, fear is a liar, and its purpose is to keep you from experiencing all that God has planned for you and those you love. His plans are always good. We may not understand God's plan, but rest assured they are good!

No disability or dictionary out there is capable of clearly defining who we are as a person.

Robert M Hensel
(Born with Spina Bifida)

Chapter 5

Mistakes Will Be Made... Help Please!

Today I messed up. I feel awful. I'm so embarrassed. It may not sound like a big deal to you, but I hate messing things up. I hate asking for help and then inconveniencing people because I messed up.

Okay, this is what happened. Andrew's communication device AKA iPad died. I arranged to get a loaner device until a new device gets approved. In addition to his device dying, the mount attached to Andrew's wheelchair that held his device was not a good fit. He had difficulty reaching the device because of the placement on his new wheelchair was all wrong. The young man helping us with all of this was outstanding! He ordered an attachment for the mount to allow Andrew to access the device easily and got all of the loaner device paperwork squared way. When the attachments came in, he reached out, and we set up a time for him to come out to the school and install the attachments. ALL I HAD TO DO WAS SEND THE OLD MOUNT! I didn't have to take a day off work to meet him at the office, I didn't have to leave my school and meet him at Andrew's school. ALL I HAD TO DO WAS SEND THE MOUNT!

Welp! Guess what your girl did? I forgot to send the old mount. In my mind, I thought he ordered a new mount, but he didn't. So, this young man drove across town with the attachments ready to get Andrew's device mounted and ready to go, only to find no mount.

I had an adult tantrum when Andrew's assistant principal texted me asking about the mount. A full-on adult tantrum. I was swinging my arms, stomping my feet, face all torn up, and screaming on the inside. Ugh! I can't stand it when I make a mistake, especially when it inconveniences others and affects Andrew.

I'm supposed to be helping to solve problems, not cause them!

As you can see from this snapshot of my perfectly imperfect life, I am the complete opposite of perfect. Nothing about me is perfect or even close. I am not a perfect person, parent, or teacher. I don't talk, think, or act perfectly.

I spent about half a decade trying to be perfect. I almost drove myself insane. I was already a little touched, but this relentless determination to be the perfect mom was a whole other level of crazy. It was so unrealistic and unfair to me and family.

Perfect for what?

Perfect for who?

What does perfect even mean?

Is your version of perfection based on what someone else views as perfect?

It is unrealistic to apply those standards to your situation. It's time to reevaluate your standards. I loathe standardized tests. In my opinion the test only measures which students are good test takers (which I'm not and most people aren't). These tests don't give any meaningful data about the students' progress or growth. They don't improve performance in the classroom setting. It only stresses students out, and makes them feel inadequate when they don't achieve a certain score. These tests and scores are a complete waste of time that we can never get back! Not to mention they are sexist, racist, and classist.

Okay, I'm getting off my soap box now. I said all of that to say, we hold ourselves to a standard that doesn't even apply to us. And at the end of the day, holding yourself to these standards causes you to be blind to all of the wonderful progress and accomplishments you have made being the amazing imperfect parent that you are.

We are going to get it wrong more often than not. Society's obsession with perfection will drive anyone insane. What is portrayed in the media is fantasy. Yet, we hold ourselves to these standards, which are cruel and unfair. We don't take into consideration our unique children and circumstances.

Let me ask you a question, who planned on being a parent of a child with unique abilities?

I'll wait.

Just as I suspected, no one. Most of us had no clue beforehand that we would have a child with different abilities. Even if we did, we would still be ill-prepared for what was ahead of us. So, we are thrown into this unknown world, network of people, language, and processes that are foreign to us. We must learn as we go. And yes, there are support groups, blogs, books, websites, and all kinds of resources, however everyone's journey is unique. Ultimately, we are trying to figure out our special situations with the help of resources and support. Still, we believe we must make the right decisions to take care of, and advocate for our child daily without a mistake. Are you hearing the crazy?

My faux pa I mentioned at the beginning of this chapter, was just one of many examples I could have given. But, let me tell you how it all worked out. When I reached out to the young man with all my apologies, he responded with "No worries, I'll be back on your side of town tomorrow. I can take care of Andrew tomorrow."

Mistakes will be made. You will forget, and say the wrong thing. You will show up to the right appointment on the wrong day. You will show up to the right appointment on the right day at the wrong time. You will show up to the right meeting, at the right time, on the right day, at the wrong place. I have done all of these things and have lived to tell about it!

However, every time I made a mistake it was okay. Earth did not fall of its axis! That's how we feel, right? I was frustrated, deflated, sometimes crying and out of breath when I would show up to the appointments. But the amount of unexpected grace I was given when facing the reality that I am not the perfect parent, was freeing. I could breathe and tell myself, "You are fine, my child is fine, we made it here safely, everything is fine." Sometimes, I would have to reschedule the appointment and that is just a consequence of showing up on the wrong day at the right time, because your appointment was the day before.

Stop laughing!

That walk of shame is not joke, but everything is fine!

Honestly, I could have avoided some of the mistakes I made if I had asked for help or accepted the assistance offered to me. One of the hardest things for this control freak to do is get help. I should also add annoyingly independent, headstrong, and downright prideful to the list. **I hate asking for help**, for anything, but especially when it comes to Andrew. Now, my reasoning is twofold. One of the reasons I don't like asking for help is because it makes me feel weak and vulnerable. I know it sounds crazy, right? But it does. I don't want anyone to know that I don't have my stuff together or that I can't handle this life.

We as parents have to appear to have it all together, right? By asking for help, it makes me feel like I'm incompetent and not enough for my kids on my own. I also don't want to be disappointed when I ask for help, and the person doesn't come through and do what they promised. Or they do things their way, which isn't the right way because it isn't the way I would have done it. Of course, my way is the only way for Andrew. I'm taking deep breaths and shaking my head as I type this. It sounds ridiculous when I read what was a part of my thinking for so long. I don't know about you but being in control makes me feel safe. It is my happy place. Because of the uncertainty in raising and caring for a special needs child, if I can control even the tiniest thing, it gives me a sense of peace, safety, and certainty in my complicated and unpredictable life.

The other reason is not wanting to be a burden or inconvenience to anyone. Instead, I would rather figure it out or not participate. I can't count the number of times the boys and I didn't go to an event or missed a cool opportunity because I didn't want to inconvenience or bother anyone because I needed an extra pair of hands to make the experience accessible for Andrew. I still feel that way sometimes. It is so selfish and unfair for all of my boys. I'm getting better, but it is still a struggle for the control freak, independent, prideful parts of me.

I must remind myself of these things when I feel myself not wanting to ask for help:

What asking for help **doesn't** mean:

1. You are incompetent.
2. You can't handle the demands of being Andrew, Austin, and Asher's mother.
3. You are weak.
4. You are not courageous.
5. You are lazy.
6. You are inconveniencing or bothering someone.

What asking for help **does** mean:

1. You are very courageous.
2. You are willing to do whatever it takes for Andrew, Austin, and Asher.
3. You are very smart and resourceful to utilize the help being offered to you.
4. You are building community.

5. You are allowing someone else to feel blessed and empowered by helping you.

I had a student this past year, we will call her Gabby (this is not the student's real name, I have never had a student named Gabby and I would never divulge the identify of any of my students), who had low muscle tone and struggled to put her backpack in her cubby as a part of our class morning routine. She would just stand at the cubby with her backpack on the floor in front of her. Gabby would attempt to pick her backpack up and put it on the hook but would fail every time. She was very stubborn and tenacious. My desk was close to the cubbies, so I observed her attempts every morning. And every morning I would ask, "Gabby, do you need some help?" She would reply vehemently, "No!" I would eventually have to intervene, or she would be standing there until the end of the school day. Even though I would intervene I would do so by placing my hands over her hands as I helped her put her backpack away. My goal was for Gabby to be able to ask for help and then eventually do it on her own.

For weeks, Gabby refused to ask for help. She would just stand there struggling until someone intervened. I told her all she had to do was ask for help. I felt so bad for her. She was missing out on morning play and social time with her friends because she refused to ask for help. I modeled what she should say, "Help, please?" But she refused. Stubborn little person!

One morning, one of the other little girls in the class who had become her best friend was playing on the carpet in class with one of their favorite toys. When Gabby came in, she spotted her immediately and you could tell by the look on her face she was anxious to join her friend. But she had to put her backpack in her cubby. She was on the Struggle Bus trying to get that backpack in her cubby. With tears in her eyes, she turned to me and said "Help, please?" I jumped out of my seat so fast and ran over to help her! With her newfound freedom of asking for help, she skipped over to her friend and began to play. From then on, Gabby would still come in and attempt to put her backpack in her cubby. When she would realize she couldn't, she asked for help. Gabby eventually became strong enough to put her backpack in her cubby independently. However, she also learned that asking for help in the meantime would get her to her friend and toys much faster.

Gabby is so much like me! I will ride that Struggle Bus until the wheels fall off. With all my independence and pride as fuel. Going nowhere fast. Something as simple as asking, "Help, please?" can be one of the hardest things to do. I get it! We don't want to be a burden or inconvenience to anyone. We don't want to seem as though we can't handle things. We always have our proverbial "SUPER MOM" cape on.

Did you see how I was watching and waiting for my opportunity to help?

I just needed her to ask for help. I didn't want to overstep or be too pushy. I also wanted her to learn it is okay to ask for help and the benefit of asking for help.

What I want you to understand, just as I was watching and waiting for my opportunity to help there are people out there waiting to help you. They don't want to overstep or be too pushy. They are just waiting for you to ask for help. So, take off your cape for a few seconds and ask someone to help you.

Say it with me..." Help, please!"

"When you focus on someone's disability you'll overlook their abilities, beauty and uniqueness. Once you learn to accept and love them for who they are, you subconsciously learn to love yourself unconditionally."

— Yvonne Pierre
(Author and mom of child diagnosed with Down Syndrome)

Chapter 6

Struggle Bus= SPED Parent Life

It was a Saturday, and simply put, I did not feel like parenting. Seriously, I was not into being a mother or a responsible adult. I didn't want to get up and make breakfast. I did not want to change a diaper, give a wipes bath because the diaper leaked, or change the linen all before 6 am. I did not want to hear the words mom, mama, mommy, or the horn on the wheelchair. I did not want to take Andrew to therapy. I did not want to cook, and puree Andrew's meal and then wait to eat because I needed to feed Andrew first. I did not want to do any of it today. I was driving that struggle bus at 1 mph. Just inching along.

You know what, honestly there are days that I don't want to drive the struggle bus. I don't want Jesus to just take the wheel, I want him to:

- Take my keys
- My driver's license
- My registration
- My van payment
- My maintenance schedule
- Let me get in the backseat and look out the window!

And you know what, that's okay. It is quite normal, which isn't a word I think I have ever used to describe myself or life. However, all the different feelings are normal. Usually, I would have needed a whole moment having these feelings. And then the lies would start:

- You aren't a good mother. A good mother would never say or feel this way about her life and motherhood.
- You are ungrateful. So many women would love to have your life and children.
- You are so lazy. Get it together.
- You are so selfish. Remember you died when your children were born. It is no longer about you. It's all about them.
- You failed all of your boys because you couldn't make your marriage work.

  I blamed myself for not being a stay-at-home mom and homeschooling my boys for years. If I had been able to make my marriage work and stay home as we had planned, they wouldn't have to be in public school. I would be able to teach them and support their strengths and interests, especially with Andrew. In my mind, he would be so much further along in academics and life if he was home with me.

- You don't deserve your children. They deserve better than you.

The list goes on and on. I could write a whole book full of the lies I have told myself over the years. But that's just what they are, LIES.

So now let's look at the truth:

- I am an outstanding mother. I am not a perfect mother. I make plenty of mistakes, but I try every day to do what is best for my boys, and I love them with all my heart.
- I thank God daily for my children. I understand how blessed I am to have one child, and God blessed me with three amazing little people! God trusted me. Knowing me, God still decided it was a good idea for me to be their mother. For that, I am grateful!
- Lazy? I am the complete opposite of lazy! Real-talk people, I wake up at 4:30 a.m. I don't stop until 10:30 p.m., and that is an early night for me. The majority of the time, my loved ones make me stop and rest,

or my body will make me stop and rest. I prefer option #1, but sometimes I am hard-headed and don't listen, and you know the rest.

- Selfish? Once again, I'm the complete opposite. Every thought, action, decision, and grocery list is made with my boys in mind. If it is not beneficial for them or will harm them somehow, it does not happen. Now, I had to learn that I am still yet alive and but, I am learning to still honor my life without feeling guilty, and I did not die when my boys arrived. My life simply, well, not simply, changed. It changed, and so did I.
- My marriage failed, but I didn't fail my boys by ending my marriage. I'm not going to share details about my failed marriage because that's my business, and that's not what we are here for. I will say, ending my marriage was a win for me and my boys. There is no lie from hell that will convince me otherwise! Am I a stay-at-home mom? Do I have to opportunity to homeschool my boys? NO! but, God has allowed us to have fabulous educational experiences thus far. I'm thriving in a profession where I can provide for my family. I have the flexibility and schedule to be with them on their days out of school, holidays, and summers. God has also allowed me to raise my boys in a safe, God-fearing, loving home. WINNING!
- God created my boys and me for each other. I could never have more perfect boys, and they could never have a mother more perfect for them.

We didn't get to choose. We were divinely placed together. I hold on to this truth when I feel like I am failing them or that I'm not enough.

We chose friends, spouses, partners, employers, houses, cars, and even shoes. However, I believe God decides when it comes to who will be parents and who their children will be, even with adoption. He doesn't make mistakes.

So, when you wake up some mornings just not feeling it, and feel like you can't do **it**, whatever **it** is one more time. It's okay. Have your moment or two. Own those feelings, then get back on the bus and parent. Your children need you!

"Being disabled should not mean being disqualified from having access to every aspect of life."

Emma Thompson

(Diagnosed with depression)

Chapter 7

Boss Up!

I have been fortunate to have a career as a Special Education Teacher. The past six years as an educator have been my best years. I teach from the perspective of an educator and a parent of a child with special needs. It makes a HUGE difference. I can advocate for my son and students with a unique knowledge. I also try to support and educate my students' parents. My biggest advice for parents is to educate themselves and proceed with caution.

So many times, I walk into an IEP (Individualized Education Plan) meeting with parents who don't have a clue. They are simply going through the motions of the meeting. Before the meeting I send a draft IEP home for parents to review and jot down questions or concerns about the document determining their child's school services. Often, parents don't even look at it. They just trust that the school district, administrator, and teachers have their child's best interest in mind and take care of them while at school.

Insert: Long pause, head cocked to the side, lips pursed and turned up, exasperation in my eyes.

As long as it does not cost the district too much money or inconvenience administration and teachers, you should be able to trust that all will be well. What you must understand is that teachers are overworked and underpaid! There is a teacher shortage everywhere because of this. Teachers work long hours at school, and most take work home on nights and weekends. Now teaching is an altruistic or selfless profession. Most teachers are not there for the paycheck. However, we all have to live, and need to rest. Because of that, the "extra mile" teacher is becoming few and far between. That teacher who will spend her last dollar at the dollar store so her students can have a wonderful learning experience is a dying breed. You can't assume the school district, administration, and teachers will tell you everything you need to know and do everything your child needs to succeed.

MINI IEP BOOTCAMP

An IEP is a legally binding document. Whoever signs that document by law is bound to carry out what the IEP states. So, your school district, administration, and teachers have to do what that document says, **period**. You are a part of the IEP team. Your input is valuable, essential, and should be heard and taken seriously. Here are some things to consider when getting ready for your next IEP meeting:

- You are the BOSS.

You are the customer, and what do they say about the customer? "The customer is always right!" Now I don't advise you to go into the meeting like, "Listen, I'm the B.O.S.S. in here, and ya'll will do whatever I say PERIODT!" Don't do that! But please understand your role in the meeting. It can be intimidating walking into an IEP meeting with at least five people sitting at the table who know more about this process than you do. They probably just had a debriefing meeting right before this meeting to develop a strategy for the meeting you are about to have. (Ask me how I know! I've been there, done that.) So don't go in meek and timid. Hold your head up, look everyone in the eye, smile, and come in educated and prepared for the meeting, LIKE A BOSS!

- Read the IEP before the meeting.

This is so important! Let the case manager know that you expect a draft IEP at least two days before the meeting. This is the law and protocol for IEP meetings. Suppose you don't receive the draft IEP before the meeting. In that case, you have the right to reschedule the meeting because you were not allowed sufficient time to read the IEP and prepare for

the meeting. The IEP contains a lot of jargon and special education terminology. It is a legal document. I suggest having a friend read over it with you. You must make friends with people in the same boat paddling with you. Also, make sure you have friends that have made it to the other side! We can't all be in the same struggle boat! It is so much easier to go through unchartered territory with someone who has "been there, done that" or is going through the same things you are. Two are better than one. You can put your heads together and do amazing things for your children. If you haven't found that type of support yet, or maybe you need a third pair of eyes to help you comb through the draft IEP, many organizations are there to help you. If your child is receiving any services or has a caseworker outside of school, they can connect you with the right people. If that is not an option for you, Google your state's special services department and tell them what you need. They will point you in the right direction. You can also Google, "How to find help figuring out the IEP process in my area?" or something along those lines. YouTube is also a great resource. Help is out there! Get a clear understanding of the IEP before the meeting. It makes a huge difference when an informed parent walks into or logs into a meeting. It's called RESPECT!

- **Hire an advocate.**

Hiring an advocate is an excellent option if you feel uncomfortable going into the meeting alone, feel unprepared, want someone at the table on you and your child's side, or to speak on your behalf. Not that the district, administrators, and teachers are not on you and your child's side, but they don't necessarily have a personal stake in the meeting. They are looking at data and behavior. Some of them have personally met your child, and some have not. Special education advocates provide independent support to people who feel they are not being heard. They help parents ensure a child's special needs are met, ensure that parents are taken seriously, and their rights are respected. In addition, advocates help parents access and understand information and services. For example, special education advocates make parents aware of available services, they go over test results and explain everything in layman's terms. They will also work with schools to plan individualized education programs (IEPs) and attend IEP meetings.

- **Know what you want for your child and be willing to fight for it.**

As a special education teacher, I have seen this far too many times. Parents will either have unrealistic expectations or very low expectations of their child. Or they have no idea what they want for their child's education and leave it up to the school. Take the time to think about what you want for your child long-term. Do you see your child getting a diploma, learning a trade, or getting a certificate? Do you think the least restrictive environment for your child is inclusion or mainstreaming? Mainstreaming is when your child is in a regular classroom for part of the day. Do you want your child to be in a special education classroom for the entire day?

Whatever you decide, bring it up at the meeting if the team doesn't. Talk about what you want and why? If the team is giving you push back, then you push back! They should at least be willing to try it for a few weeks to see how it goes. If you feel strongly about it, keep pushing until you get results. This is also where a special needs advocate would come in handy.

Now, please do not come to the meeting with a list of unrealistic demands or goals for your child that you know are unobtainable. You know your child. I would not go into a meeting asking Andrew's teachers to allow him to answer questions or make a comment during every class period. It takes a while for Andrew to respond using his device. Not because he doesn't have an answer or doesn't know what to say, but navigating his device takes time for him. So, I wouldn't ask his teachers to allow him to answer questions or give a response daily. I would ask them to offer the opportunity at least once a week because I know my child. Do I want him to get to the point where he can answer questions daily? Yes! When he gets there, we will add that to his IEP. Until then, we will be realistic. I have been in so many IEP meetings that have ended with a plan that makes the parent happy, but not necessarily a plan that reflects their child's ability and need.

- **Research, Research, Research!**

Research children with the same diagnosis as your child. Search for blogs of parents with children with the same or similar diagnosis. You can even reach out to those parents on the blog and ask for advice. You can use your research to find out what other children similar to your child are doing in school. You can find out what model they are using, curriculum, behavior modifications, and effective techniques. Parents of children with special needs are some of the most creative and innovative individuals I have ever encountered. We don't just make lemonade out of lemons. We make lemon squares, lemon custard, lemon meringue pie, lemon drop candies, and lemon cookies, leaving everyone shocked and in awe at how we did so much with so little. Remember: Just because it hasn't been done before doesn't mean it can't be done! The answer will always be "no" until you ask, then "no" means you ask a different way until they say "yes." Listen, if you come into the meeting unprepared, with no research, and "in your feelings", you will be perceived as one of those crazy SPED moms. However, if you come into the meeting with research-based evidence and data supporting what you are requesting, the rest of the team is more willing to listen and try something new.

- **Take notes or ask to record the meeting.**

You cannot remember everything discussed and decided in the meeting. Someone will take official notes at the meeting, and you will receive a copy. However, you will want your version and interpretation of what was said. So, at the beginning of the meeting, ask if it is okay that you record the meeting. Most schools will have no problem with that and will probably pull out a device to record the meeting.

- **Meet for however long you need to meet, and meet as many times as you need to meet.**

Remember you are not here to make friends, win the school's "Kindest Parent Award," or make the school faculty's job easier. You are there to advocate for your child and ensure they have the best education possible. Don't worry about inconveniencing anyone. This is a part of their job description. Remember, you are fighting for your child who doesn't have a voice. Your purpose is to ensure your child receives FAPE (Free Appropriate Public Education) in an LRE (Least Restrictive Environment). I have been in a 6-hour IEP meeting before with one bathroom break! The parent apologized at the end for keeping us so long, but she was not leaving until everything on that IEP was the way she wanted it. Sometimes you have to be **THAT PARENT**! I hate to see **them** coming, but I have nothing but respect for them.

So, **BOSS UP**, my friends! Get in there and get it done! At the end of some of my meetings for Andrew, I want to get up, walk to the door, reach in my purse, pull out a mic, turn around, drop it, and walk away

LIKE A BOSS!

"Your success and happiness lies in you. Resolve to keep happy, and your joy and you shall form an invincible host against difficulties."

—Helen Keller
(Born blind and deaf)

Chapter 8

Take Care

Take Care

I was driving to work one morning. Let me rephrase that. I was flying down the interstate like a highly skilled Nascar Driver. I woke up late because I didn't wake up at 3am like I do every morning to use the bathroom. I got in bed around 11pm and had no idea when I finally fell asleep. I usually run on about 3.5 to 4 hours of sleep a day. I was looking like Casper the Friendly Ghost because I am severely anemic and needed a blood transfusion. But who has time for that, right? So, I take ten supplements a day, enough iron to set off a metal detector, and blood pressure medication. As I type this, I have three vitamin patches on my back. Chile, can you say **STRUGGLE BUS**!?

This didn't all start today, this week, or even this month. It comes from months, dare I say, years of neglecting myself and "pushing through" because I don't have time to be sick, take breaks, or relax. I know for sure that if you don't take care of yourself, your body will make you.

"Mom or Dad Guilt" is real, and I think it is even more real for parents of children with special needs. How dare I have friends who put up with my crazy and hang out! Let's not talk about laughing and cutting up with them. That is a "No, thank you!" Going away for the weekend without "The Three Wise Men" in tow? I should be ashamed of myself to entertain the thought!" Don't even get me started desiring to be in a loving relationship with someone. These three boys can love me, and no one would be interested in taking part in this crazy life. My heart has reached its capacity and can't be broken by disappointment and rejection again. Also, dating someone would take precious time away from caring for my boys. Chile, that's another chapter, maybe.

In my dramatic, highly imaginative brain, I am convinced that taking care of myself and having fun, or having a meaningful, loving relationship outside of my family will not allow me to take care of my children properly. The time that I'm using to go to dinner with a friend, get a massage, take a walk, or even take a quick nap should be used to do something with Andrew. We could be doing exercises, stretches, homework, practicing talking with his device, etc. There is always something to be done. Not just with Andrew but also with Austin and Asher. I spend so much time taking care of Andrew that I feel guilty about not spending enough time with them. So, if I have extra time, I must use it to make up for all the time that I didn't spend with them because I was taking care of Andrew.

Now that my body is a hot mess, I'm having to be retroactive instead of proactive. I want to encourage you to take care of yourself. I am still learning this, so I'm writing this for myself too. People always tell me, "You need to take some time for yourself," or "Girl, you need a spa day!" I look at them and say, "When and how am I supposed to secure childcare for this spa day?" It's not like I can hire a teenager or college student with five stars from Care.com and go to the spa for a few hours. I need specialized care for Andrew. I know respite is out there for families, but you have to qualify for it. Then finding a good respite provider and working around their schedule is a headache, which brings me to **FORGET IT**! The problem is, I can't forget it. I can't forget about taking care of myself physically, mentally, and emotionally, or I won't be well enough to care for my boys. That's the last thing I want.

Parenting is exhausting, but let's be honest, parenting a child with special needs is five to ten times more demanding. It requires more time, energy, thinking, patience, as well as strength to get through a day. The stress level of a special needs parent is high (find research). When we as parents push through the warning signs, because we don't have time to go to the doctor or are too busy going to our child's appointments, we do more harm than good. Many times, I have said, "I don't have time to be sick! I just have to keep it moving. This will pass." But it doesn't pass. The symptoms may subside, but they usually return with other more severe symptoms. This is why I am writing this chapter from the "Struggle Bus."

Here are some ideas that I have tried in the past. They were suggested to me, and I need to revisit them. We are all a work in progress. I am not writing this book to suggest I have it all figured out and I'm perfect, so you need to listen to me. Nor am I suggesting I'm winning in every area of my life especially when it comes to parenting a special needs child. I am writing this book to say to any parent of a special needs child, you are not alone. I'm in the same boat with you, trying my best to stay afloat.

Self-Care Ideas:

1. While your child is at therapy, go outside- walk, listen to music in the car, read a book, get a smoothie or coffee, strike up a conversation if another parent is in the waiting room.

2. Have a private dance party at home or in the car whenever you need a quick pick me up. Research shows that music can affect our emotions in different ways. Happy, upbeat music causes our brains to produce chemicals like dopamine and serotonin, which evoke feelings of joy. In contrast, calming music relaxes the mind and the body. In my opinion, music is one the best de-stressors in life! Who needs Xanax when you can play Maze featuring Frankie Beverly and have "Happy Feelins" in the air? I'm so glad God created music. It gets me through most of my days. Research also shows that music can lower blood pressure and cortisol levels, AKA the stress hormone. If you listen to classical music like Beethoven or Chopin, it has been found that it will lower your cortisol levels. Even if classical isn't your thing, put it on for a little bit to calm down. It's better than having a stroke or heart attack while listening to Marvin Gaye or Maroon 5 (just saying). Consider putting together a playlist for those stressful moments or days and turn it up when you need a pick me up. Doing this for 5 to 6 minutes a day could help you manage your stress level.

3. Don't feel like partying: take a 5-minute gratitude meditation or do some gratitude journaling. I know you don't need one more thing to do, but it will shift your perspective and give you peace and hope on your worst day. When you look for things to be thankful for, you find them. Even the tiniest thing like my kid drank out of a straw today without choking. You can probably think of something else like I had a good hair day. Oh! Or my youngest son didn't have a meltdown for the five millionth time because his brother beat him in a race, and I didn't burn the oatmeal this morning! Or… we almost made it to school on time, only 3 minutes late instead of our usual 8! One of my students mastered a goal! I was able to get everything on my grocery list. (Lord, there have been some moments at check out when I have had to hold up the line putting items back one by one based on necessity until I reached my predetermined budget.) And my mom said that she was going to make dinner on Friday, so I don't have to cook after work on Friday! You see how that works. I try to do this before I go to bed at night, and it cleanses my mind of all the ugly and helps me focus on the good. This helps me wind my mind down much more quickly, which allows me to fall asleep faster. Go get yourself a pretty journal, fancy pen, and say, "Thank you!"

4. Letting trusted people in your circle prevent feeling depressed, lonely, overwhelmed, and isolated. This circle doesn't have to be super big. I can't handle having a lot of people in my circle because it requires too much time and energy. I can count on one hand how many people I purposefully spend time with regularly outside of my family. When you allow this to happen, you can use time with them to take care of yourself. For example, you can ask them to come over and watch your child while you take a nap if you don't feel comfortable leaving the house. They can sit and watch a movie with your child while you go for a walk around the neighborhood. If you trust this person, you can schedule a spa day! What I like most of all is making arrangements to go and hang out with my people. A change of scenery or atmosphere can do wonders for your mood and outlook. The Bible says a merry heart does the body good like medicine. This is so true. After a few hours of cutting up with my people, I come back home feeling lighter, more patient, happier, and more

relaxed. Your child needs you to be this person regularly, and your body needs a break from the stress you inflict upon it daily.

6. Do the things you enjoy doing. You don't always have to leave the house. Having to stay home for months with my "Three Wise Men" has taught me so much about staying sane when you can't leave. My boys can handle being without me in their face for at least an hour and a half to two hours, AKA the length of a movie. I would make sure they had eaten, and snacks were available for the younger two. They need to eat every hour even if they just had a full meal. Boys! I change Andrew and make sure he is comfortable, so caring for him is not on my mind. I turn on a movie or a television show that I approve of and go to my room. I have two closets in my room, and I converted the largest of the two into an office. It was one of the best remodeling decisions I have made. When in the office, I can barely hear the movie, so I can shut out the extra noise. During this time, I do the things that I like to do. I enjoy Paint by Numbers, Diamond Art, journaling, listening to music, and looking at Facebook. I sing and dream, or literally dream when I get in bed and take a nap. When I emerge from my room, I am refreshed and ready to cook the next meal. BOYS!!!

The bottom line is, take care of yourself! No matter what you decide to do, make a conscious effort to put yourself first. I don't want anyone else taking care of my children, and I don't want anyone to have to take care of me in addition to my children. If I don't want any of those things to happen, I must do what I can to prevent it. Stress disables and takes people away from their loved ones daily. I don't want to become a statistic, and I don't want my children to become one either. I had to understand that I was being selfish, irresponsible, and a horrible mother when I didn't take care of myself. When I do the things, I need to do to be my best for my boys, we all win!

"Use the skills that I have got. Do not focus on what I have not. Of course, I am aware of my limitations. Yet, I am a part of God's wonderful creation."

-William E. Lightbourne

(Blind)

Chapter 9

Enjoy the Moments

I enjoy lying on the floor while Andrew plays in my hair, binge-watching seasons of cooking shows on Netflix, laughing uncontrollably at Christian comedy, and singing and dancing around the room. Walking into the living room on Sunday morning to see all three boys watching church service on the television brings me joy. When I asked how Andrew got in here, my middle son Austin answered, "I pulled him in here, but I asked him the whole time if I was hurting him, and he said, "no". That was an answered prayer, and my day was made!

We love swimming in the pool on a hot summer day, singing and dancing to our favorite songs in the van. Movie night cuddled together on the corner of the sectional, watching our favorite movies for the 15th time is priceless. Family vacations with aunts and grandparents, teaching mommy how to ride the hoverboard and watching her fall, getting caught in the rain, and then deciding to stay outside and play in it! The smiles, the laughter, the hugs, the memories. Write them down, take lots of pictures, and reminisce every chance you get. You will need this during challenging times.

I remember being so stressed out and anxious about the boys' upcoming school year. So much change was taking place. Andrew and Austin were going to a new school without me! This was the first time since they were school age that they would not be in the same educational institution as me. They would be entering 5th and 6th grade at an intermediate school. My nerves, Lord! In addition, my youngest, Asher, was accepted into the Escolars Academy at a different elementary school. Of course, I requested a transfer to his new school. Unfortunately, the only position available was a grade level I didn't have any experience with. That meant everything was new for all of us! My nerves, Lord, my nerves! I felt so out of control.

Enjoy the Moments

Once again, I'd entered the land of the unknown. I tried to plan, but I had no idea what to plan for. My boys never attended an intermediate school. The faculty and staff did not have any experience working with a child with Andrew's different abilities. No one knew Andrew, and up until the day before school started the district hadn't found an adult support to assist him in navigating his day at school. Asher will now go to a completely different school with the only familiar face being Mommy's. Still, I'm on the other side of the school.

The school year happened, and we survived. We did more than survived, we thrived! My new position at Asher's new school was a dream! It was the exact change I needed, and I was so happy with my move. Asher did great at the new school. He adjusted and made new friends. He quickly became his teacher's unspoken favorite. Austin adjusted well at his new school too. He started there not knowing anyone except Andrew. However, Andrew was in 6th grade, so he never really saw him. Austin did a great job making friends and becoming more aware of his strengths and weaknesses academically. He made some adjustments and finished the year on the A Honor Roll! He did encounter some challenges on the bus with bullying, but he persevered and never changed his character. He is stronger and more confident after overcoming those incidences. Andrew, well he totally exceeded everyone's expectations. Once the teachers were able to get to know him, they loved him and did everything they could to help him succeed. He had an amazing team, and his paraprofessional was heaven sent! She did so much along with his resource teacher to facilitate learning and support Andrew and his teachers.

Throughout this school year, I had to remind myself of all the good moments and my whys. When Andrew came home with skin scraped off his knuckles because he didn't clear a doorway completely. I had to take deep breaths and ask myself:

Did he die? No.

Is he okay? Yes.

Does this happen often? No, it was the first time.

Is there a plan in place so it doesn't happen again? Yes.

Then, I must move on and think about the picture I just got of him participating in science class or his progress report showing he is making favorable progress on all goals and subjects. When I had a hard day in my new class with my new students, Asher would come bursting through my classroom door chatting about something new he learned in class, or to stump me with a new riddle he came up with walking to my classroom. No matter the challenges of my new position, Asher is why I am here. When Austin came home upset because he was bullied on the bus, he stood up for himself and was proud. I looked at his strength and confidence and reflected on how much he grew and matured this school year.

It all comes back to your perspective. What are you going to choose to focus on? No, you can't just look through rose-colored glasses all day and pretend nothing is going wrong and there aren't challenges in your life. However, you can choose your response to those challenges, and you can choose where your thoughts dwell. Will you obsess over all of the difficult situations you have to deal with, or will you handle things as they come while enjoying your present and reflecting on great memories you have had.

If you have a hard time remembering in the hard moments like I sometimes do, keep a journal, take pictures, get a tattoo. Have something that you can refer to when you need to be reminded of all the wonderful things that have happened in your life that outshines the present mayhem that is trying to destroy your child, family, and sanity. At least it seems that way. Remember to be present when you have those sweet pure bliss moments. Those memories will carry you to the next moment.

I am different but not less.

-Temple Grandin

(diagnosed with Autism)

Chapter 10

But I Love it Here!

But I Love it Here

We stayed home again today. It was summer break and we have been home all week. My younger boys were about to drive me and each other crazy. The only sane person in the house was Andrew. So why had we been home all week? It wasn't because of Covid. It's not because one of us was sick. It's not because of a lack of transportation. It's not because my boys just wanted to stay home. It was me. It's all me. I didn't want to get ALL the things together to go somewhere (diapers, wipes, extra clothes, snacks, drinks). I didn't want to wrestle with the new chair and put another hole in the wall. I didn't want to deal with the "pity" stares, the "eww gross he's drooling" stares, the "Lawd, she look so tired and weary" stares, the "little kids" stares, or just "the stares." I didn't want to deal with Andrew running into clothes racks (new chair again) and almost running people over then laughing about it (his humor is sometimes inappropriate). I can't deal with his slow-motion driving when I am always full speed ahead. My other two angels constantly fighting and asking for everything they see (even though they were told not to ask me for anything when we get in the store). They never bring money but want the whole store! Writing this makes me want to stay home for another week.

I call this self-induced isolation because I choose to stay home and not deal with doing uncomfortable things. I allow myself to do this from time to time. I create my bubble and I am content with me and my three. I'm naturally introverted, so it serves me well. However, all of my boys are **EXTRAverts** and crave interaction with others. Thankfully, they have each other, but they get on each other's nerves the way brothers do. Quite honestly, Andrew is not amused by his brothers most of the time. He would rather engage with adults or teenagers (he's so mature for his age, mercy!).

So, with all of that being said, I can't remain in my self-induced isolation for long. It isn't healthy for my boys or me.

BUT I LOVE IT HERE!

It feels safe, and I can protect them and myself from this cruel world. I can control the environment and use less words (my favorite!). All the things that make me happy. **Protect them, be in control, and use fewer words!**

However, this is not sustainable or healthy. So, I venture out into the world at least twice a week, especially in the summer. Doing this meets my boys' needs and the needs of others we encounter. These people may not know they need a dose of the Phillips crew, but they do! Everyone needs to see our unique family. We are incredible, precious, EXTRAORDINARY, valuable, and beautiful. We are also, **LOUD**, silly, **LOUD**, accident-prone, **LOUD**, and **LOUD**!

Andrew is also terrifying behind the joystick of his motorized wheelchair. He catches you off guard. You will see Andrew coming down the aisle at you in his chair, showing no signs of veering to the left or right until the last second right before hitting you for his amusement. Yes, he does it for the laughs and to embarrass me. He just laughs as I apologize profusely to the woman who just jumped out of the way to save her toes, ankles, and shins. However, I guarantee you she will be prepared the next time she sees him or someone else in a wheelchair coming her way. We are doing the world a favor, preparing, and educating people one store at a time!

Over 5.5 million wheelchair users are in the United States (Cloud of Good Website). That's a lot of people! So, we can't stay home and act as if our kids don't exist or not allow them to figure out how to navigate in real life and be as independent as possible. I also believe that the more our family is out and about, the more normalized it becomes.

Seeing people with service animals in stores, restaurants, and airports was shocking at first. I remember the first time I saw a little dog in a shopping cart with a work vest on. I was like, "Oh dear, could she not have left him in the car with the window down?" I am highly allergic to pet dander, so I was like, "No! This is not okay! I will have a sneeze attack for five minutes with running itchy eyes and nasal congestion because this woman thinks it's cute to bring her little puppy with its little vest into the store!" That was my ignorant, uninformed compassionless reaction to something that I knew nothing about. Now I smile and politely push my cart to another aisle and mind my business. I understand the need, and I'm used to seeing service animals everywhere. I know how to handle myself to make sure the person with their service animal and I are comfortable. If these people stayed home, self-isolated, and weren't willing to endure the negative ignorant reactions, I wouldn't be the well-adjusted and evolved person I am today. At least when it comes to service animals. I'm a whole project for God in other areas of my life.

Frankly, when the boys and I are out and about we make businesses aware of the lack of accessibility of their establishments. When shopping in department stores and trying to get down the aisles when there are clothing racks everywhere is very difficult. So either, I have to move rounders out of the way and mess up the store's configuration of clothing or I request to speak to management...it depends on how much time I have. When brought to management's attention, they are always very apologetic and thankful that I brought it to their attention. However, when dining at restaurants… mercy! Just navigating to a table is a **WHOLE OBSTACLE COURSE!** The restaurant is only concerned about how many tables they can cram into a space so they can serve as many patrons as possible. They do not take into consideration how wide the aisle needs to be for a wheelchair.

I don't run into these issues often because we choose to stay home. In my opinion it is very rare that restaurants have patrons in a wheelchair that must be accompanied. Therefore, it is not a common practice to accommodate. Therefore, I have patience for these establishments when we are out and about. I believe the problem is two-fold. For businesses, if you stay ready you don't have to get ready. It is required by law that your establishments meet ADA standards and be accessible to all patrons. We don't want any more attention on us. When businesses must get ready for us, it makes us feel unwelcomed and discourages us from continuing to come out and enjoy our communities and businesses. For us as parents, if we would be more visible in our communities and businesses, they would stay ready.

So, get your hot mess of a family out of the house. I don't care where you go, just go! You can go grocery shopping, to the library, to the mall, go to the playground, go to the zoo, or go for a walk around your neighborhood. **Be the reason businesses have to stay ready!** Don't stay in the house and keep your child hidden like they are a secret. They are a gift to be shared!

It may very likely be a hot mess, but at least you are trying. And guess what I have seen plenty of "typical" kids act out and do all kinds of wild and crazy things outside of the house. Their parents get embarrassed and must get themselves together as well as their child. Some parents just drop everything and run out of the store with their child too embarrassed to continue their shopping trip. Other parents just continue shopping and ignore their child's behavior as if they hear or see nothing. I have also seen the parent who engages their child who is acting out and gets the behavior under control and then continues shopping. Either way, who cares?!?!?!? Let them look and even stare! Let them form their own opinions. Their ignorance and opinions have nothing to do with you or your child. Everything isn't going to be peaceful and calm all the time. Everyone needs to learn how to embrace diversity and uniqueness.

No more hiding.

No more excuses.

Not tomorrow, today.

Get up and Get out!

"It is our culture that disables. When one is disabled, the problem is not really that they have impairments and social skill deficits. The issue at stake is that they live in an 'ableist' culture that rarely affords them the space or opportunity to make their unique contribution to society and does not lift up the value of choosing them as friends."

-Ben Conner

(Director of a Centre for Disability and Ministry at Western Theological Seminary)

Chapter 11

The World Needs More Scarlets

Go out to eat, go shopping, go to amusement parks, swimming, and to playgrounds. Your child will enjoy these experiences, and they will desensitize the world. Everywhere we go, people stare. They are always polite, but you can tell that they are uncomfortable with having Andrew there. Uncomfortable and unsure, but not in a bad way.

People are uncomfortable because it is not often that a child with special needs comes into a restaurant or store driving a wheelchair with a communication device attached and unbothered. I can count the number of times I have seen a child with cerebral palsy in a public place other than an event or establishment explicitly designed or organized for people with special needs. So, I understand how if one is not used to seeing a person in a wheelchair, especially a child, it can emote some uncomfortable feelings. The staff is often unsure about what to do or say. They seem uncertain if they should speak to Andrew, give him a pound, look at him, or just pretend he isn't there. Then there is the question of how they will accommodate him. In restaurants, they move tables and rearrange things. It is a whole production. We are often offered seating in the back of the restaurant. Well, we all know that isn't acceptable for many reasons. I can understand if his wheelchair will be in the way or if we are with a large party and the larger tables are in the back of the restaurant. However, if I feel that they have us in the back to make sure other patrons are not offended or made to feel uncomfortable, let's just say that never goes well.

Most of the time, we are welcomed and accommodated by staff who are teachable and more than willing to do whatever they can to make Andrew's experience enjoyable. The more we are out and about in the community, the more comfortable we all will be with differences.

To be fully transparent, I'm usually uncomfortable and freaking out when we are out and about, especially when going to a new restaurant or store. Any new unchartered territory makes me incredibly anxious. Not because I don't know what to do or understand his needs. It's the stares. The "deer caught in the headlights" look when we approach to be seated. It's the possibility of being turned away because Andrew's chair can't make it into a building because it is old, and the makeshift ramp at the back of the restaurant would potentially damage his chair or be dangerous for him. It's the uncomfortable questions that no one asks about my other two boys. "What happened to him?" Kids ask the best questions. "What's wrong with his legs? Why is he in a wheelchair? Why does he have that iPad on his chair? Why can't he talk?" or just a confused stare. Kids don't look away.

Although I have been answering these questions for years and have a whole script, I still get butterflies in my stomach. I still have to pause and fight tears sometimes because I wish I didn't have to answer these questions. Not that I want Andrew to be different, but that Andrew being out and about in the community wasn't so rare that it causes people to stare and ask questions. With the growing number of children with disabilities, seeing a child with a disability should be more normalized. I still get a little angry only because I'm not asking you, "Why is your child having a full tantrum on the floor, but you are concerned about why my child is in a wheelchair?" I'm wondering, "Why did you wear that shirt with those pants because it makes me uncomfortable?" but I dare not ask you.

I also feel happy and thankful for the questions. Instead of just staring, someone is taking a moment to acknowledge that Andrew is a person. They genuinely care about what is going on with him.

The boys and I went to an accessible park one summer. A handful of children were already there playing and running off some of that energy. All three boys took off the moment they got through the fence. I always let Andrew explore and zoom around in his chair to give him some independence. Of course, I have my eyes on all of them the entire time, and I'm close by if needed. A little girl named Scarlet was at the park with her dad and brother. When she saw Andrew zooming around the playground, she immediately took interest. Andrew wanted to get out of his chair and get on the zip line swing thing (my best description), but Scarlet was on the swing. I told Andrew he had to wait his turn. When she saw us waiting, she got off and came over. I asked her if she was done because Andrew wanted to give it a go. She said, "Sure!" and asked if she could help him get in. I told her I got it, but thanks. Then the questions began, she was so sweet and innocent about it. First, she wanted to know his name and then what had happened to him. Scarlet was straightforward and matter of fact with her questioning. It was almost as if she was collecting data for a report she would be working on later. Then she started sharing some things about herself as she gave unsolicited assistance in pushing Andrew. She stayed with Andrew for the rest of the time we were there.

Scarlet was eight years old, after I explained to her that he was a twelve-year-old trapped in his body and he understands everything you are saying and wants to talk and hang out with you, they were chatting it up in their own way. It amazed me how comfortable and at ease she was around him. Scarlet shared with me that she often gets picked on at school because sometimes she gets lice and has to cut all her hair off, and it is hard for her to make friends. She told me that anytime she sees someone different or like Andrew, she makes friends with them because she knows how it feels not to have friends. "He's just a kid, like me! All kids want a friend." She is an amazing little girl, and I told her so. I wish there were more Scarlets in the world.

Once you choose hope,
anything's possible.

-Christopher Reeve

(Spinal Cord Injury)

Chapter 12

Love is Waiting

Rejection and the unknown are two of my biggest fears concerning Andrew and myself. The looks he gets when we are out and about living our best life vary from, "Oh, you poor thing" to "Ewww, he's drooling!" Either way, they try not to make eye contact when passing. isn't everyone, fear wants me to believe that everyone sees Andrew and myself this way. Fear tells me that no one will accept us, want to get to know us, or love us. Honestly, we get more smiles and hellos than "Oh, you poor thing" and "Ewww, he's drooling!" looks. People are generally kind, and little kids are just curious. But do I listen to the truth? I'm getting better with the truth as time goes on.

I experience love from others who could not care less that I have a child with different abilities and those who love that I have a child with different abilities.

The majority of my friends have issues. I don't think they mind me saying so. I believe that is why we hang out because we make each other feel normal. Let me clarify my statement, "the majority of my friends." That statement makes me sound like a social butterfly or Miss Popularity. That is not the case. I can count on one hand those who are close to me outside of my family.

Nevertheless, we all have issues, and our children have problems. For some reason, I had convinced myself that I was the only single mother who had a child with different abilities. No one would understand my life or want to be around my children and me. I honestly believed that there wasn't anyone who would genuinely want to be friends with me. This is what happens when you isolate yourself. You lose perspective and start imagining things that aren't rational or realistic. Since you are alone with your thoughts, you don't have anyone around to give you a different perspective or challenge those thoughts. Once those thoughts begin, you go down the proverbial rabbit hole, where your thoughts keep getting darker and darker. Eventually, those thoughts become a false reality, and you become stuck in that reality.

I never dreamed that my life would be like this. I dreamt of playdates, story times at the library, and meeting for brunch while the children play. My children were going to be involved in the community and sports. I dreamed of sitting on the park bench chatting with other moms while our children ran around and played. Not my reality.

So, making friends or even opening myself up to friendships was a losing battle in my mind from the beginning. Whenever anyone approached me and struck up a conversation at the library or playground, I automatically thought they were curious about Andrew. They were coming over to check their "charity box" by making small talk with the poor mom of the child with special needs and two other boys. I couldn't see that someone would want to be my friend and would adore my boys.

Well, guess what? I was wrong! The fear of rejection was lying to me and keeping the boys and me trapped in isolation. Sure, we were out and about shopping, going to the movies, eating at restaurants, and enjoying vacations. But we were always in our little bubble.

My first real friend was unexpected. We worked together and bonded over the crazy that was going on at our place of employment. Talking to her was easy. She was nonjudgmental and kept talking to me even after meeting my boys and witnessing snippets of my life. We didn't scare her away! I didn't scare her away. Then she invited me to get something to eat outside of work! Say what?!?!? Did she really want to hang out with me?

I tried to keep the conversation light and not get too heavy. I was afraid to let her glimpse the crazy lurking underneath the smiles and the enormous sense of humor. But for some reason, I felt like she knew, and I couldn't believe that she still wanted to hang out with me! Well, news flash! I wasn't the only one on the planet with hard stuff, and my day-to-day life of caring for my boys encourages and inspires others unbeknownst to me. This life that I'm living that I think no one would ever want to be a part of is a life that many are intrigued by and want to know more about.

Imagine that! The fear of being rejected and the need for self-isolation to protect my boys and me was a lie. I'm walking around inspiring people and didn't even know it. Talk about a perspective change.

As I began to open up more and more with my friend, I began to let go of those anxieties. She shared with me how I inspire her and so many other people. Not inspire like, "aww, look at the poor single mom with the special needs kid. Her struggle is so inspirational." More like, "Wow, look at her! She is a boss! I have no idea how she does this every day and still smiles and has something positive to say. If she can do this, then I can too!" She tells me all of this, and I'm like, "who me?!?" You never know who is watching and who you are impacting by just living your life. So on those days you are genuinely struggling and don't want to try anymore, remember, your struggle could be someone else's breakthrough.

When I finally started letting people into my life and Andrew's life, I began to see his ministry. No one has ever been the same after encountering Andrew. He always lifts their spirit. They leave him feeling encouraged and blessed to have met him. And he doesn't say a word. The anointing within him speaks to their soul through his beautiful smile and gestures. Don't deny others of your child's gift.

After my divorce, I convinced myself that I was unlovable, and no one would come within 10 feet of me. A man wouldn't want to get to know me with three young boys, including one with special abilities. Who would want to get involved with a woman who had all this baggage? We're not talking about the baggage that leaves the nest after a few years, but baggage that may stay for decades. I wouldn't get involved with me. I'm tired all the time. I'm always tending to Andrew and my other boys. I get a break on most Friday nights, and their dad gets them every other Saturday night and brings them back on Sunday. I drive an hour one way each time to drop them off and pick them up, so that isn't much of a break. When would we even have time to get to know each other?

So, I decided I would date when I could, but I would never get my hopes up because I knew I would be rejected. I always gave off the "I'm unlovable, so don't even try" energy. Only someone with x-ray vision to see the fragile heart deep inside, strong arms to hold me, and a gentle and caring spirit to understand the complexity of my life and accept all of my boys as they are would do. He needed a strong stomach to deal with the smell of poopy diapers, a sense of humor, and strong shoulders so I can cry when I need to. A strong back to lift Andrew and hold me up when I'm tired. My children and I needed someone with a strong will and hands who will do whatever it takes to ensure we are okay and have what we need. He must be fearless, fight alongside me hand in hand, and have a great heart. It must be a love that will see past my flawed, dramatic, layered self. All I will say is that God sees, hears, and is able! Wink, Wink! Chile, let me move on because ya'll are trying to get me to tell my business!

You aren't a burden; your child isn't a burden. The people who want to be in your life and are ordained to be there will see the blessing.

They will love you and your child and see them as beautiful gifts. It's okay to let people experience and enjoy you and your child.

So, allow yourself to be loved and cared for. You deserve love, and you don't have to do extra to receive love because you have a child who requires more love and care. There are so many times I have closed myself off from people because I felt like, "Who would want to be my friend? We can't have regular playdates. Their kids can't play with my son like they would with other kids. I don't want to make anyone feel uncomfortable or even obligated. I don't want a pity friendship. I wanted to protect myself and Andrew from all the scenarios I had in my head that would hurt him or me.

I spent years in isolation. When I gave birth to Andrew's younger brothers, they were birthed into the same isolation. I thought I was protecting us. Instead, I was depriving us of love and life. You are worthy of unconditional love. You are extraordinary and full of love. You are a blessing, and your life is a blessing. Allow others to experience that blessing.

When you have a disability, knowing that you are not defined by it is the sweetest feeling. In My Dreams, I Dance

-Anne Wafula Strike (contracted Polio at two, resulting in the diagnosis of below t7 paralysis)

Chapter 13

Dream a New Dream

Dream A New Dream

Close your eyes, and no peeking! For real, close your eyes and take a deep breath. Now focus on your child with different abilities. Are you smiling? I know every time I think of Andrew, I smile. Okay, now think of how amazing they are and how they have beaten the odds so many times. Think of all the things the doctors, specialists, and therapists said your child wouldn't be able to do. Think about how your child proved them wrong again and again.

Think about your dreams, all the hopes, and plans. Let that dream play out. Think about your child running and playing on a playground. See your child picking flowers and running up to you saying, "Here, I picked these for you!" Think about them playing soccer, basketball, or golf. See them walking into their school and they turn around waving goodbye with a huge smile on their face before the enter into the school to start their day.

Imagine yourself daydreaming one of those fantastic straight-out-of-a-movie dreams, one of those dreams that seem so real you can even smell the flowers and taste the salt in the air. Have you ever had one of those dreams? And then suddenly, you wake up confused because you are not sure if what you were dreaming was a dream or if the events happened in real life. You feel disappointed that it was only a dream and that your reality is nothing like your dream. That's how it feels when you hear that your child has been diagnosed with Cerebral Palsy, it's like waking up from a beautiful dream. You don't want to believe it. You want to go back to sleep, live in your dream world with your child, and your family to live happily ever after.

I used to dream about Andrew a lot when I was still carrying him. I had so many dreams for this little person. He would be intelligent, athletic, and love

God with all his heart, mind, and soul. Andrew was going to make us proud. But, when faced with the diagnosis of cerebral palsy, it's hard to see how your dream could ever become a reality. How did my dream become a nightmare? I know that doesn't sound good, but it's how I felt. I felt like I woke up from a beautiful dream to a nightmare. All of my hopes and dreams were thwarted.

But this is where perspective plays a part once again. All of my dreams have come true and then some! This guy is so intelligent. Is he athletic? No, but he can go really fast in his chair and has a need for speed. He is a great driver now, so I think if he were to play or get into a sport, it would be race car driving or drag racing. And boy, does this boy love God with all his heart, mind, and soul. He loves watching Pastors preach, always asks his Oma to read the Bible to him, and loves to watch gospel concerts, as well as Christian comedians. He hates to miss church and loves to pray. Andrew has a light that shines so bright in him that anyone with eyes and a soul can see it. Anyone who spends time with him is never the same. My mom tells him all the time to smile because his smile and laugh are his ministries and gifts to the world. When you see that smile and hear his laugh, you can't help but smile and laugh with him. Laughter is healing, and we all need some healing. He is a wonderful gift and has changed many lives by being Andrew. Talk about exceeding my hopes and dreams.

What I saw as a nightmare has become a beautiful dream. Ha! Who am I kidding, it is a dream. Sometimes it's a nightmare that I wish someone would wake me up and rescue me from. Sometimes it's picture-perfect, and I never want to wake up. It's life and life has ebbs and flows. It is nothing like my original dream for Andrew, but whose kid comes out and fulfills all of their dreams?

So, your dreams didn't come true, and your child won't be the doctor, lawyer, teacher, star athlete, husband, wife, mother, or father you dreamed they would be. Now what? You can see every day as a nightmare and a constant reminder of unfulfilled dreams, or

You can dream another dream.

Dream A New Dream

It's okay to do that, you know. It's okay to let go of one dream to dream another dream. We all have to do that at some point. It is not easy, but it is necessary to heal, grow, and live a life of peace and joy. Sometimes you have to let go of the old to embrace something new fully.

I went to a trampoline park with my two younger boys once. They had doctor appointments, and I tried to treat them to activities we wouldn't ordinarily do if Andrew was with us. We had a blast! We were bouncing all over the place and having uninhibited fun. It was much needed. The park is divided into different sections, and one of the sections has foam pits with various obstacles you have to go through to cross the pit. Well, of course, my boys wanted me to try the obstacles. I told ya'll before I'm a girly girl control freak. I was okay with bouncing on the trampoline, but this foam pit was another level of love I had to tap into. I had to dig deep!

So, I decided I would cross this pit using the foam balance beam. It had two ropes hanging from the ceiling to help me balance. At least, that is what they were supposed to do. I stepped onto the beam and held on to the rope for dear life. Lord, I was hollering and calling for my boys to help me! You would have thought snakes and alligators were in the pit. I took one tentative step after the other, holding on to the rope for dear life. My hands were sweating and slipping. I kept stepping until I got to the middle of the beam. The rope wouldn't reach any further. The only way I would be able to move forward is to let go of the rope behind me and take hold of the rope in front of me. So many thoughts ran through my mind:

- What if I fall into the pit? If I can't reach and hold on to the rope in front of me, I could fall into that nasty foam pit. Have you ever fallen into a foam pit? It is like sinking into quicksand, and it is so hard to get out of. I didn't want to go through that! Not again!

- I could reach out, hold on to the rope, start taking steps, then run out of rope again and get stuck.

- Or I could do all of step 2, and instead of getting stuck, I could jump. If I jump, I have a 50/50 chance of making it.

I reached, and I fell! Ya'll, I fell in that nasty spongy ball pit, and it took me five minutes to get out with the help of Austin and Asher. I was exhausted when I finally climbed out, partly because of how hard it was to get out and partly from laughing so hard at my failed attempts to get out. After getting my wind back, I got right back on the foam balance beam. I fell again. Yes, my stubborn, tenacious, this is not going to beat me behind, got right back on that foam balance beam from Lucifer's house, and this time I made it! I used a combination of step 2 and step 3 .

Sometimes you must let go of what's behind you to move forward toward what is in front of you. Do you see what I did there? Let the old dream go. It is no longer applicable, and that is okay.

Let go, look ahead, and dream a new dream.

We all have expectations and dreams for ourselves, our children, family, friends, and coworkers. However, these expectations must be realistic and attainable. In so many ways, I have had and still have unrealistic and unattainable expectations of myself. It's not fair to me, and it isn't fair to our children with different abilities. So why do we hold on to this unrealistic and unobtainable dream of how our children will be and what they will become?

The majority of dreams are unrealistic, that is why they are called dreams. But often times they give us hope and something to hold on to. You know I'm right.

The "dream" child I described earlier in the chapter, was a product of books, magazines, movies, and people I've talked to and observed. This society has unrealistic and insane standards and images that we believe our children and we ourselves must reach. It's not fair to put our unrealistic dreams and expectations on any child, especially those with different abilities. And then, when they don't meet our expectations or make our dreams come true, we look at them with disappointment and embarrassment. We repeat this cycle with every lost dream, failure, or disapproval. Your child can feel the hurt and disappointment, more than you know. It doesn't feel good, and it isn't fair.

We must look to God and the Holy Spirit to guide us and give us wisdom and insight on how to lead, teach, and dream.

I have been guilty of lowering my expectations of Andrew at times because I wanted him to succeed, and I didn't want to be embarrassed or disappointed. In my mind, I think that if I set the bar low, he will knock it out of the water, and I will feel like I'm doing well as a parent. The expectations had nothing to do with Andrew's ability or well-being. These expectations had everything to do with validating me as a parent. Uh oh, I'm really telling my business now. It is the ugly, sad truth of the matter. We will lower our expectations of others to avoid disappointment, control a situation or person, and keep others dependent on us. That was not a read; it was real. It's ugly and messy, but it's real. I'm going stop while I'm ahead because I feel like I am in somebody's business. Let me just sit that on the table over here and move on before you decide you want to return your book!

Keep dreaming, keep hoping, and keep believing… Tweak those dreams as needed to fit who you are dreaming about. And if possible, ask your child what their dreams are. You will be surprised what they are dreaming of doing with their lives.

Andrew was given an assignment in his sixth grade English/Language Arts Class. He had to read a poem about someone's dream and then write a poem about his own dream.

The first stanza describes his unique characteristics. The second stanza describes his dream, not necessarily defines it. The third stanza describes the things that make him great.

Andrew used his communication device to share his dream and I typed them.

Here is Andrew's Dream!

My Dream

By: Andrew Phillips

My dream is the color of my skin,
my arms and legs,
my mouth.

It's the thing that makes me special,
but not the thing
that makes me great.

The first time I used my arms
to get me where I wanted to go,
the passion I have for music
and appreciation of
the smiles I see every time
I belly laugh.

CPSIA information can be obtained
at www.ICGtesting.com
Printed in the USA
BVHW050455100323
660081BV00012B/989